The Sardonic Humor
of
Ambrose Bierce

Edited by
George Barkin

Dover Publications, Inc.
New York

Published in Canada by General Publishing Com-
pany, Ltd., 30 Lesmill Road, Don Mills, Toronto,
Ontario.
Published in the United Kingdom by Constable
and Company, Ltd., 10 Orange Street, London
WC 2.

This Dover edition, first published in 1963, is
a new collection of verses and prose sketches by
Ambrose Bierce, selected from *The Collected Works
of Ambrose Bierce*, published by the Neale Publishing Company in twelve volumes between 1909
and 1912.

Standard Book Number: 486-20768-4

Library of Congress Catalog Card Number: 63-19487

Manufactured in the United States of America
Dover Publications, Inc.
180 Varick Street
New York, N.Y. 10014

PREFACE

This new collection of verse, fables, satirical essays and stories by Ambrose Bierce is designed as a companion volume to his delightful *Devil's Dictionary*. Although the short pieces included here reveal the same mordant wit that made the *Dictionary* a classic of American humor, they have not enjoyed the general currency of that famous work. Originally published in part in newspaper columns and long unavailable though included in the twelve-volume *Collected Works*, they are now republished by Dover Publications, Inc., as a special treat for the ever-growing audience of Bierce enthusiasts.

A legend in his own lifetime, Bierce was born in a log cabin in 1842 in Meigs County, Ohio, self-educated at his father's small library, and exposed to man's inhumanity to man in some of the most arduous campaigns of the Civil War. It was while he was working at the San Francisco Mint that some of his short pieces—pungent paragraphs in the *Argonaut* and *News Letter* pinpointing human foibles—began to attract attention. A long career of journalism and letters, including the writing of the "Prattle" column for the Hearst *Sunday Examiner*, followed. In 1913, disillusioned and weary, he disappeared into Mexico after notifying friends, "If you hear of my being stood up against a Mexican stone wall and shot to rags please know that I think it a pretty good way to depart this life." While many legends persist, the story of his last days has never been told.

Bierce wrote in the tradition of Swift, attacking the corrupt social institutions of his time and addressing his work to those "enlightened souls who prefer dry wines to sweet, sense to sentiment, wit to humor, and clean English to slang." While many persons were stung by his trenchant comments on mankind, few could deny the clarity of observation behind them. The pieces included here—selected from *The Collected Works of Ambrose Bierce*, published from 1909 to 1912 in twelve volumes by the Neale Publishing Company—constitute some of the best examples of that vision. The fact that the same pomposities and hypocrisies exist today in much the same form makes these verses and prose sketches especially pertinent today. It is to be hoped that this new selection of Bierce's work will bring enlightenment and delight both to those who know and love Bierce and to those who may be discovering him for the first time.

CONTENTS

Selections from *Shapes of Clay*

Contents

Contents

Selections from *Aesopus Emendatus*

Selections from *Negligible Tales*

The Parenticide Club

Selection from *The Fourth Estate*

Selections from *The Ocean Wave*

Selections from *Tangential Views*

Selections from *The March Hare*

Selection from *Antepenultima*

Selection from *The Sample Counter*

Selection from *In Motley*

The Sardonic Humor

of

Ambrose Bierce

SHAPES OF CLAY

POLYPHEMUS

'Twas a sick young man with a face ungay
  And an eye that was all alone;
And he shook his head in a hopeless way
  As he sat on a roadside stone.

"O, ailing youth, what untoward fate
  Has made the sun to set
On your mirth and eye?" "I'm constrained to state
  I'm an ex-West Point cadet.

" 'Twas at cannon-practice I got my hurt
  And my present frame of mind;
For the gun went off with a double spurt—
  Before it, and also behind!"

"How sad, how sad, that a fine young chap,
  When studying how to kill,
Should meet with so terrible a mishap
  Precluding eventual skill.

"Ah, woful to think that a weapon made
  For mowing down the foe
Should commit so dreadful an escapade
  As to turn about to mow!"

No more he heeded while I condoled:
 He was wandering in his mind;
His lonely eye unconsidered rolled,
 And his views he thus defined:

" 'Twas O for a breach of the peace—'twas O
 For an international brawl! *rear part of the*
But a piece of the breech—ah no, ah no, *bore of gun*
 I didn't want that at all."

RELIGION

Hassan Bedreddin, clad in rags, ill-shod,   *hypocrisy*
Sought the great temple of the living God. *protecting*
  The worshipers arose and drove him forth, *the beautiful*
And one in power beat him with a rod. *temple from*
                                        dirty

"Allah," he cried, "thou seest what I got:
Thy servants bar me from the sacred spot."
  "Be comforted," the Holy One replied;
"It is the only place where I am not."

VISIONS OF SIN

*Kraslajorsk, Siberia.—My eyes are better, and I shall travel slowly
toward home.—Danenhower.*

From the regions of the Night,
Coming with recovered sight—
From the spell of darkness free,
What will Danenhower see?
He will see when he arrives
Doctors taking human lives.
He will see a learned judge
Whose decision will not budge
Till both litigants are fleeced

And his palm is duly greased.
Lawyers he will see who fight
Day by day and night by night;
Never both upon a side,
Though their fees they still divide.
Preachers he will see who teach
That it is divine to preach—
That they fan a sacred fire
And are worthy of their hire.
He will see a trusted wife,
Pride of some good husband's life,
Enter at a certain door
And—but he will see no more.
He will see Good Templars reel—
See a prosecutor steal,
And a father beat his child.
He'll perhaps see Oscar Wilde.

From the regions of the Night
Coming with recovered sight—
From the bliss of blindness free,
That's what Danenhower'll see.

    1882.

GENIUS

What is the thing called Genius? One has said
   'Tis general ability directed
Into a special channel. One, instead,
   Proffers a definition much respected
By toiling dullards: genius, he explains,
Is infinite capacity for taking pains.

Max Nordau, seeing he has not the thing,
   Has solemnly decided, with Lombroso,
That genius is degeneracy. Ring
   The curtain down—the show is only so-so;

I'd rather see a dog-fight than sit out
This inconclusive definition-bout.

What, then, is genius? Faith, I'm only sure
    That I am deep in doubt about the matter;
But this I *think:* of two in literature
    He is the greater genius who's the fatter.
'Twas in an age less prosperous that those
Were kings of thought who starved by verse and prose.

Lo! the lean rhapsodist whose soul surveys,
    Ecstatic, his unprofitable vision,
Interprets it in cleanly speech; arrays
    His jeweled words with scholarly precision!
Faith, he's a dunce or he would never lack
The means to wedge his belly from his back.

'Twere passing easy to allay his pang
    Had he the genius—that's to say, the insight
Commercial. If he would but sing in slang
    He'd earn the wherewithal to make his skin tight.
Genius (let's now define the word afresh)
Is the capacity to take on flesh.

Spirit of Letters, hail! Thy reign is Now;
    Thy ministers are gentlemen that waddle—
Children of light and leading who avow
    They swap, for tallow, speech that's not a model,—
For laminated kidney-suet trade
Unsavory words. You must be stout, George Ade.

ARMA VIRUMQUE

"Ours is a Christian army"; so he said
A regiment of bangomen who led.
"And ours a Christian navy," added he
Who sailed a thunder-junk upon the sea.
Better they know than men unwarlike do

What is an army, and a navy too.
Pray God there may be sent them by-and-by
The knowledge what a Christian is, and why.
For somewhat lamely the conception runs
Of a brass-buttoned Jesus firing guns.

ARTHUR McEWEN

Posterity with all its eyes
Will come and view him where he lies.
Then, turning from the scene away
With a concerted shrug, will say:
"H'm, *Scarabæus Sisyphus*—
What interest has that to us?
We can't admire at all, at all,
A tumble-bug without its ball."
And then a sage will rise and say:
"Good friends, you err—turn back, I pray:
This freak that you unwisely shun
Is bug and ball rolled into one."

CONTEMPLATION

I muse upon the distant town
   In many a dreamy mood.
Above my head the sunbeams crown
   The graveyard's giant rood. *crucifix*
The lupin blooms among the tombs,
   The quail recalls her brood.

Ah, good it is to sit and trace
   The shadow of the cross;
It moves so still from place to place
   O'er marble, bronze and moss;
With graves to mark upon its arc
   Our time's eternal loss.

And sweet it is to watch the bee
　　That revels in the roses,
And sense the fragrance floating free
　　On every breeze that dozes
Upon the mound, where, safe and sound,
　　Mine enemy reposes.

THE JACK OF CLUBS

Jerome, you are a mighty famous man—
　　District Attorney, I believe they call you.
Some shout your praise as loudly as they can,
　　And some, apparently, just live to maul you.
　　But whether good or ill repute befall you,
Your critics can't deny that, as a rule,
　　You take it standing—though the wits among
Them say you stand, as does the singing mule,
　　The better to perform your feats of lung.
And, truly from the dawning to the gloaming,
When in good voice, you're usually Jeroming.

O, well, we must have music—'tis a need,
　　Like Ibsen, Shaw or the "Edenic diet";
Though sometimes silence is desired—indeed,
　　There's much that may be said in praise of quiet,
　　And possibly you might do worse than try it.
'Twere better, anyhow, than fool advice
　　To the police to club their fellow men,
Too sore already. Sir, it is not nice
　　To free your snouty virtues from the pen—
Unless, as once in Gadara, they'll scamper
Down a steep place to where 'tis greatly damper.

Jerome, the best of us are those who care
　　To hide from view the monsters that inhabit
Our hearts, and when too closely questioned swear
　　We've nothing fiercer than a sheep or rabbit.
　　Seeing an opportunity, you grab it

And lifting up the curtain, show the whole
  Menagerie of thoughts and feelings which
Infest the secret places of your soul
  Like newts and water-puppies in a ditch.
O, great reformer! hide from observation
The unpleasing spectacle of Reformation.
  1905.

ANOTHER ASPIRANT

George Dewey, dear, I did not think that you—
So very married and so happy, too—
Would go philandering with another girl
And give your gay mustache a fetching curl
And set your cap—I should say your cocked hat—
At Miss Columbia the like o' that.
Pray what can you expect to get by throwing
Sheep's eyes at one so very, very knowing?

See how she served McKinley! All his life
He wooed her for his morganatic wife,
Swore that he loved her better than his soul
(I'm half inclined to think, upon the whole,
She better did deserve his love), then vowed
He'd marry her alive, or even aloud!
What did she? Ere his breath he could recover
She heartlessly accepted that poor lover!

There's William Bryan of the silver tongue,
Old in ambition, in discretion young—
He courts her with the song, the dance, the lute,
But knows how suitors feel who do not suit.
And Teddy Roosevelt, plucking from its sheath
The weapon that he wears behind his teeth,
Endeavors in his simple, soldier fashion,
But all in vain, to touch her heart by slashin'.

Beware, my web-foot friend, beware her wiles:
Fly from her sighs and disregard her smiles.
She's no fool mermaid with a comb and glass,
But Satan's daughter with a breast of brass.
Put out your prow to sea again—but hold!
If Bryan and McKinley, all too bold,
Show up along the beach with little Teddy—
Well, Dewey, you may fire when you are ready.
April, 1900.

AFTER TENNYSON

You ask me why, though ill at ease,
   Within this region I subsist,
   Where honor's dead, and law is hissed,
And all men pillage as they please.

It is the land where freemen kill
   In warm debate their party foes;
   The land where judges come to blows
And speak the things that make us ill;

A land of base expedient;
   A land where gold can justice drown;
   Where Freedom's chains are handed down
From President to President;

Where factions wrangle for the bread
   Of honest men; where, fearing naught,
   Accurst monopolies have caught
The people in the nets they spread;

Where branded convicts execute
   The laws that in a better time
   They broke, and every kind of crime
Stalks unashamed and resolute.

Should honor e'er possess the land,
 And patriots control the State,
 And Justice rise, divine with hate,
To choke the politician band,

O waft me from the harbor forth,
 Wild winds. I'll see Alaska's sky.
 Here 'twill have grown too warm, and I
Will run for office in the North.

BUSINESS

Two villains of the highest rank
Set out one night to rob a bank.
They found the building, looked it o'er,
Each window noted, tried each door,
Scanned carefully the lidded hole
For minstrels to cascade the coal—
In short, examined five-and-twenty
Short cuts from poverty to plenty.
But all were sealed, they saw full soon,
Against the minions of the moon.
"Enough," said one: "I'm satisfied."
The other, smiling fair and wide,
Said: "I'm as highly pleased as you:
No burglar ever can get through.
Fate surely prospers our design—
The booty all is yours and mine."
So, full of hope, the following day
To the exchange they took their way
And bought, with manner free and frank,
Some stock of that devoted bank;
And they became, inside the year,
One President and one Cashier.
Their crime I can no further trace—
The means of safety to embrace,
I overdrew and left the place.

"THE WHOLE WORLD KIN"

"Liars for witnesses; for lawyers brutes
Willing to lose their souls to win their suits;
Cowards for jurors, and for judge a clown
Who ne'er took up the law, yet lays it down;
Justice denied, authority abused,
And the one blameless person the accused—
Thy courts, my country, all these dreadful years,
Move fools to laughter and the wise to tears."

So moaned an alien from beyond the foam.
Come here, my lad, I think you'll feel at home.

THE HESITATING VETERAN

When I was young and full of faith
   And other fads that youngsters cherish
A cry rose as of one that saith
   With emphasis: "Help or I perish!"
'Twas heard in all the land, and men
   The sound were each to each repeating.
It made my heart beat faster then
   Than any heart can now be beating.

For the world is old and the world is gray—
   Grown prudent and, I think, more witty.
She's cut her wisdom teeth, they say,·
   And doesn't now go in for Pity.
Besides, the melancholy cry
   Was that of one, 'tis now conceded,
Whose plight no one beneath the sky
   Felt half so poignantly as he did.

Moreover, he was black. And yet
   That sentimental generation

With an austere compassion set
    Its face and faith to the occasion.
Then there were hate and strife to spare,
    And various hard knocks a-plenty;
And I ('twas more than my true share,
    I must confess) took five-and-twenty.

That all is over now—the reign
    Of love and trade stills all dissensions,
And the clear heavens arch again
    Above a land of peace and pensions.
The black chap—at the last we gave
    Him everything that he had cried for,
Though many white chaps in the grave
    'Twould puzzle to say what they died for.

I hope he's better off—I trust
    That his society and his master's
Are worth the price we paid, and must
    Continue paying, in disasters;
But sometimes doubts press thronging round
    ('Tis mostly when my hurts are aching)
If war for Union was a sound
    And profitable undertaking.

'Tis said they mean to take away
    The Negro's vote for he's unlettered.
'Tis true he sits in darkness day
    And night, as formerly, when fettered;
But pray observe—howe'er he vote
    To whatsoever party turning,
He'll be with gentlemen of note
    And wealth and consequence and learning.

With saints and sages on each side,
    How could a fool through lack of knowledge,
Vote wrong? If learning is no guide
    Why ought one to have been in college?
O Son of Day, O Son of Night!
    What are your preferences made of?

I know not which of you is right,
  Nor which to be the more afraid of.

The world is old and the world is bad,
  And creaks and grinds upon its axis;
And man's an ape and the gods are mad!—
  There's nothing sure, not even our taxes.
No mortal man can Truth restore,
  Or say where she is to be sought for.
I know what uniform I wore—
  O, that I knew which side I fought for!

TO-DAY

I saw a man who knelt in prayer,
    And heard him say:
"I'll lay my inmost spirit bare
    To-day.

"Lord, for to-morrow and its need
    I do not pray;
Let me upon my neighbor feed
    To-day.

"Let me my duty duly shirk
    And run away
From any form or phase of work
    To-day.

"From Thy commands exempted still,
    Let me obey
The promptings of my private will
    To-day.

"Let me no word profane, no lie,
    Unthinking, say
If any one is standing by
    To-day.

"My secret sins and vices grave
  Let none betray;
The scoffer's jeers I do not crave
  To-day.

"And if to-day my fortune all
  Should ebb away
Help me on other men's to fall
  To-day.

"So, for to-morrow and its mite
  I do not pray;
Just give me everything in sight
  To-day."

I cried: "Amen!"   He rose and ran
  Like oil away.
I said: "I've seen an honest man
  To-day."

THE DYING STATESMAN

It is a politician man—
  He draweth near his end,
And friends weep round that partisan,
  Of every man the friend.

Between the Known and the Unknown
  He lieth on the strand;
The light upon the sea is thrown
  That lay upon the land.

It shineth in his glazing eye,
  It burneth on his face;
God send that when we come to die
  We know that sign of grace!

Upon his lips his blessed sprite
Poiseth her joyous wing.
"How is it with thee, child of light?
Dost hear the angels sing?"

"The song I hear, the crown I see,
And know that God is love.
Farewell, dark world—I go to be
A postmaster above!"

For him no monumental arch,
But, O, 'tis good and brave
To see the Grand Old Party march
To office o'er his grave!

LAUS LUCIS

Theosophists are about to build a "Temple for the Revival of the Mysteries of Antiquity."—Vide the Newspapers, *passim.*

Each to his taste: some men prefer to play
At mystery, and others at piquet.
Some sit in mystic meditation; some
Parade the street with tambourine and drum.
One studies to decipher ancient lore
Which, proving stuff, he studies all the more;
Another swears that learning is but good
To darken things already understood,
Then writes upon Simplicity so well
That none agree on what he wants to tell,
And future ages will declare his pen
Inspired by gods with messages to men.
To found an ancient order, these devote
Their time—with ritual, regalia, goat,
Blankets for tossing, chairs of little ease
And all the modern inconveniences;
Those, saner, frown upon unmeaning rites
And go to church for rational delights.

So all are suited, shallow and profound,
The prophets prosper and the world goes round.
For me—unread in the occult, I'm fain
To damn all mysteries alike as vain,
Spurn the obscure and base my faith upon
The Revelations of the good St. John.

TECHNOLOGY

'Twas a serious person with locks of gray
    And a figure like a crescent;
His gravity, clearly, had come to stay,
    But his smile was evanescent.

He stood and conversed with a neighbor and
    With (likewise) a high falsetto;
And he stabbed his forefinger into his hand
    As if it had been a stiletto.

His words, like the notes of a tenor drum,
    Came out of his head unblended,
And the wonderful altitude of some
    Was exceptionally splendid.

While executing a shake of the head,
    With the hand, as it were, of a master,
This agonizing old gentleman said:
    " 'Twas a truly sad disaster!

"Four hundred and ten longs and shorts in all,
    Went down"—he paused and snuffled.
A single tear was observed to fall,
    And the old man's drum was muffled.

"A very calamitous year," he said,
    And again his head-piece hoary
He shook, and another pearl he shed,
    As if he wept *con amore*.

"O lacrymose person," I cried, "pray why
  Should these failures so affect you?
With speculators in stocks no eye
  That's normal would ever connect you."

He focused his orbs upon mine and smiled
  In a sinister sort of manner.
"Young man," he said, "your words are wild:
  I spoke of the steamship 'Hanner.'

"For she has went down in a howlin' squall,
  And my heart is nigh to breakin'—
Four hundred and ten longs and shorts in all
  Will never need undertakin'!

"I'm in the business myself," said he,
  "And you've mistook my expression;
For I uses the technical terms, you see,
  Employed in my perfession."

That old undertaker has joined the throng
  On the other side of the River,
But I'm still unhappy to think I'm a "long,"
  And a tape-line makes me shiver.

A REPLY TO A LETTER

O nonsense, parson—tell me not they thrive
  And jubilate who follow your dictation.
The good are the unhappiest lot alive—
  I know they are from careful observation.
  If freedom from the terrors of damnation
Lengthens the visage like a telescope,
And lacrymosity's a sign of hope,
  Then I'll continue, in my dreadful plight,
To tread the dusky paths of sin, and grope

Contentedly without your lantern's light;
  And though in many a bog beslubbered quite,
Refuse to flay me with ecclesiastic soap.

You say 'tis a sad world, seeing I'm condemned,
  With many a million others of my kidney.
Each continent's Hammed, Japheted and Shemmed
  With sinners—worldlings like Sir Philip Sidney
And scoffers like Voltaire, who thought it bliss
To simulate respect for Genesis—
  Who bent the mental knee as if in prayer,
  But mocked at Moses underneath his hair,
And like an angry gander bowed his head to hiss.

Seeing such as these, who die without contrition,
Must go to—beg your pardon, sir—perdition,
  The sons of light, you tell me, can't be gay,
But count it sin of the sort called omission
  The groan to smother or the tear to stay
  Or fail to—what is that they live by?—pray.
So down they kneel, and the whole serious race is
Put by divine compassion on a praying basis.

Well, if you take it so to heart, while yet
  Our own hearts are so light with nature's leaven,
You'll weep indeed when we in Hades sweat,
  And you look down upon us out of Heaven.
In fancy, lo! I see your wailing shades
Thronging the crystal battlements. Cascades
Of tears spring singing from each golden spout,
  Run roaring from the verge with hoarser sound,
  Dash downward through the glimmering pro-
      found,
Quench the tormenting flame and put the Devil out!

Presumptuous fool! to you no power belongs
To pitchfork me to Heaven upon the prongs
  Of a bad pen, whose disobedient sputter,
With less of ink than incoherence fraught,

Befits the folly that it tries to utter.
Brains, I observe, as well as tongues, can stutter:
You suffer from impediment of thought,
Save when considering your bread-and-butter.

When next you "point the way to Heaven," take care:
Your fingers being thumbs, point Heaven knows
where!
Farewell, poor dunce! your letter though I blame,
Bear witness how my anger I can tame:
I've called you everything except your hateful name!

TO OSCAR WILDE

Because from Folly's lips you got
Some babbled mandate to subdue
The realm of Common Sense, and you
Made promise and considered not,—

Because you strike a random blow
At what you do not understand,
And beckon with a friendly hand
To something that you do not know,

I hold no speech of your desert,
Nor baffle with porrected shield
The wooden weapon that you wield,
But meet you with a cast of dirt.

Dispute with such a thing as you—
Twin show to the two-headed calf?
Why, sir, if I repress my laugh,
'Tis more than half the world can do.
1882.

JUDEX JOCOSUS

We blench when maniacs to dance begin.
What makes a skull so dreadful is the grin.
When horrible and ludicrous unite,
Our sense of humor does but feed our fright.
As the shocked spirit with a double dread
Might see a monkey watching by the dead,
Or headsman part a neck, without a fault,
While turning o'er the block a somersault.
So, Judge Hilario, the untroubled awe
And reverence men cherish for the law
Turn all to terror when with wit profound
And tricksy humor *you* the law expound.
More frightful sounds the felon's doom by half
From lips still twisted to an idiot laugh.

TO THE BARTHOLDI STATUE

O Liberty, God-gifted—
    Young and immortal maid—
In your high hand uplifted,
    The torch declares your trade.

Its crimson menace, flaming
    Upon the sea and shore,
Is, trumpet-like, proclaiming
    That Law shall be no more.

Austere incendiary,
    We're blinking in the light;
Where is your customary
    Grenade of dynamite?

Where are your staves and switches
    For men of gentle birth?
Your mask and dirk for riches?
    Your chains for wit and worth?

Perhaps, you've brought the halters
    You used in the old days,
When round religion's altars
    You stabled Cromwell's bays?

Behind you, unsuspected,
    Have you the axe, fair wench,
Wherewith you once collected
    A poll-tax from the French?

America salutes you—
    Preparing to "disgorge."
Take everything that suits you,
    And marry Henry George.
    1894.

AN UNMERRY CHRISTMAS

Christmas, you tell me, comes but once a year.
One place it never comes, and that is here.
Here, in these pages no good wishes spring,
No well-worn greetings tediously ring—
For Christmas greetings are like pots of ore:
The hollower they are they ring the more.
Here shall no holly cast a spiny shade,
Nor mistletoe my solitude invade,
No trinket-laden vegetable come,
No jorum steam with Sheolate of rum.
No shrilling children shall their voices rear.
Hurrah for Christmas without Christmas cheer!

No presents, if you please—I know too well
What Herbert Spencer, if he didn't tell
(I know not if he did) yet might have told
Of present-giving in the days of old,
When Early Man with gifts propitiated
The chiefs whom most he doubted, feared and hated,

Or tendered them in hope to reap some rude
Advantage from the taker's gratitude.
Since thus the Gift its origin derives
(How much of its first character survives
You know as well as I) my stocking's tied,
My pocket buttoned—with my soul inside.
I save my money and I save my pride.

Dinner? Yes; thank you—just a baby's body
Done to a nutty brown, and a tear toddy
To give me appetite; and as to drink,
About a half a jug of blood, I think,
Will do; for still I love that good red wine,
Coagulating well, with wrinkles fine
Fretting the satin surface of its flood.
O tope of kings—divine Falernian—blood!

Duse take the shouting fowls upon the limb,
The kneeling cattle and the rising hymn!
Has not a pagan rights to be regarded—
His heart assaulted and his ear bombarded
With sentiments and sounds that good old Pan
Even in his demonium would ban?

No, friends—no Christmas here, for I have sworn
To keep my heart hard and my knees unworn.
Enough you have of jester, player, priest:
I as the skeleton attend your feast,
In the mad revelry to make a lull
With shaken finger and with bobbing skull.

However you my services may flout,
Philosophy disdain and reason doubt,
I mean to hold in customary state
My dismal revelry and celebrate
My yearly rite until the crack o' doom,—
Ignore the cheerful season's warmth and bloom
And cultivate an oasis of gloom.

BROTHERS

Scene—A lawyer's dreadful den.
Enter stall-fed citizen.

LAWYER.—Mornin'. How-de-do?
CITIZEN. Sir, same to you.
Called as counsel to retain you
In a case that I'll explain you.
Sad, *so* sad! Heart almost broke.
Hang it! where's my kerchief? Smoke?
Brother, sir, and I, of late,
Came into a large estate.
Brother's—h'm, ha,—rather queer
Sometimes [*tapping forehead*] here.
What he needs—you know—a "writ"—
Something, eh? that will permit
Me to manage, sir, in fine,
His estate, as well as mine.
Of course he'll storm; 'twill break, I fear,
His loving heart—excuse this tear.
LAWYER.—Have you nothing more?
All of this you said before—
When last night I took your case.
CITIZEN.—Why, sir, your face
Ne'er before has met my view!
LAWYER.—Eh? The devil! True:
My mistake—it was your brother.
But you're very like each other.

CORRECTED NEWS

'Twas a maiden lady, the newspapers say,
Pious and prim and a bit gone-gray.
　　She slept like an angel, holy and white,
　　　Till ten o'clock in the shank o' the night,
When men and other wild animals prey,

And then she cried in the viewless gloom:
"There's a man in the room, a man in the room!"
And this maiden lady, they make it appear,
Leapt out of the window, five fathom sheer!

Alas, that lying is such a sin
When newspaper men need bread and gin
    And none can be had for less than a lie!
For the maiden lady a bit gone-gray
Saw the man in the room from across the way,
And leapt, not out of the window but in—
    Ten fathoms sheer, as I hope to die!

MR. FINK'S DEBATING DONKEY

Of a person known as Peters I will humbly crave your leave
An unusual adventure into narrative to weave—
Mr. William Perry Peters, of the town of Muscatel,
A public educator and an orator as well.
Mr. Peters had a weakness which, 'tis painful to relate,
Was a strong predisposition to the pleasures of debate.
He would foster disputation wheresoever he might be;
In polygonal contention none so happy was as he.
'Twas observable, however, that the exercises ran
Into monologue by Peters, that rhetorical young man.
And the Muscatelian rustics who assisted at the show,
By involuntary silence testified their overthrow—
Mr. Peters, all unheedful of their silence and their grief,
Still effacing every vestige of erroneous belief.
O, he was a sore affliction to all heretics so bold
As to entertain opinions that he didn't care to hold.

One day—'twas in pursuance of a pedagogic plan → dogmatic
For the mental elevation of Uncultivated Man—
Mr. Peters, to his pupils, in dismissing them, explained
That the Friday evening following (unless, indeed, it rained)
Would be signalized by holding in the schoolhouse a debate
Free to all who their opinions might desire to ventilate

On the question, "Which is better, as a serviceable gift,
Speech or hearing, from the barbarity the human mind to
    lift?"
The pupils told their fathers, who, forehanded always, met
At the barroom to discuss it every evening, dry or wet.
They argued it and argued it and spat upon the stove,
And the non-committal barman on their differences throve.
And I state it as a maxim in a loosish kind of way:
You'll have the more to back your word the less you have to
    say.
Public interest was lively, but one Ebenezer Fink
Of the Rancho del Jackrabbit, only seemed to sit and think.

On the memorable evening all the men of Muscatel
Came to listen to the logic and the eloquence as well—
All but William Perry Peters, whose attendance there, I
    fear,
Was to wreak his ready rhetoric upon the public ear,
And prove (whichever side he took) that hearing wouldn't
    lift.
The human mind as ably as the other, greater gift.
The judges being chosen and the disputants enrolled,
The question he proceeded *in extenso* to unfold:
"*Resolved*—The sense of hearing lifts the mind up out of
    reach
Of the fogs of error better than the faculty of speech."
This simple proposition he expounded, word by word,
Till they best understood it who least perfectly had heard.
Even the judges comprehended what he ventured to explain—
The impact of a spit-ball admonishing in vain.
Beginning at a period before Creation's morn,
He had reached the bounds of tolerance and Adam yet un-
    born.
As down the early centuries of pre-historic time
He tracked important principles and quoted striking rhyme,
And Whisky Bill, prosaic soul! proclaiming him a jay,
Had risen and like an earthquake, "reeled unheededly
    away,"
And a late lamented cat, when opportunity should serve,
Was preparing to embark upon her parabolic curve,

A noise arose outside—the door was opened with a bang,
And old Ebenezer Fink was heard ejaculating "G'lang!"
Straight into that assembly gravely marched without a wink
An ancient ass—the property it was of Mr. Fink.
Its ears depressed and beating time to its infestive tread,
Silent through silence, moved amain that stately quadruped!
It stopped before the orator, and in the lamplight thrown
Upon its tail they saw that member weighted with a stone.
Then spake old Ebenezer: "Gents, I heern o' this debate
On w'ether v'ice or y'ears is best the mind to elevate.
Now 'yer's a bird ken throw some light uponto that tough
    theme:
He has 'em both, I'm free to say, oncommonly extreme.
He wa'n't invited for to speak, but he will not refuse
(If t'other gentleman ken wait) to exposay his views."

Ere merriment or anger o'er amazement could prevail,
He cut the string that held the stone on that canary's tail.
Freed from the weight, that member made a gesture of de-
    light,
Then rose until its rigid length was horizontal quite.
With lifted head and level ears along his withers laid,
Jack sighed, refilled his lungs and then—to put it mildly—
    brayed!
He brayed until the stones were stirred in circumjacent
    hills,
And sleeping women rose and fled, in divers kinds of frills.
'Tis said that awful bugle-blast—to make the story brief—
Wafted William Perry Peters through the window, like a
    leaf!

Such is the tale. If anything additional occurred
'Tis not set down, though, truly, I remember to have heard
That a gentleman named Peters, now residing at Soquel,
A considerable distance from the town of Muscatel,
Is opposed to education, and to rhetoric, as well.

TO MY LAUNDRESS

Saponacea, wert thou not so fair
   I'd curse thee for thy multitude of sins—
  For sending home my clothes all full of pins,
A shirt occasionally that's a snare
And a delusion, got, the Lord knows where,
   The Lord knows why, a sock whose outs and ins
    None know, nor where it ends nor where begins,
And fewer cuffs than ought to be my share.
But when I mark thy lilies how they grow,
   And the red roses of thy ripening charms,
    I bless the lovelight in thy dark eyes dreaming.
I'll never pay thee, but I'd gladly go
   Into the magic circle of thine arms,
    Supple and fragrant from repeated steaming.

FAME

One thousand years I slept beneath the sod,
   My sleep in 1901 beginning,
Then, by the action of some scurvy god
   Who happened then to recollect my sinning,
   I was revived and given another inning.
On breaking from my grave I saw a crowd—
   A formless multitude of men and women,
Gathered about a ruin. Clamors loud
   I heard, and curses deep enough to swim in;
   And, pointing at me, one said: "Let's put *him* in!"
Then each turned on me with an evil look,
As in my ragged shroud I stood and shook.

"Nay, good Posterity," I cried, "forbear!
   If that's a jail I fain would be remaining
Outside, for truly I should little care
   To catch my death of cold. I'm just regaining
   The life lost long ago by my disdaining

To take precautions against draughts like those
   That, haply, penetrate that cracked and splitting
Old structure." Then an aged wight arose
   From a chair of state in which he had been sitting.
   And with preliminary coughing, spitting
And wheezing, said: " 'Tis not a jail, we're sure,
Whate'er it may have been when it was newer.

" 'Twas found two centuries ago, o'ergrown
   With brush and ivy, all undoored, ungated;
And in restoring it we found a stone
   Set here and there in the dilapidated
   And crumbling frieze, inscribed, in antiquated
Big characters, with certain uncouth names,
   Which we conclude were borne of old by awful
Rapscallions guilty of all sinful games—
   Vagrants engaged in practices unlawful,
   And orators less sensible than jawful.
So each ten years we add to the long row
A name, the most unworthy that we know."

"But why," I asked, "put mine in?" He replied:
   "You look it"—and the judgment pained me greatly;
Right gladly would I then and there have died,
   But that I'd risen from the grave so lately.
   But on examining that solemn, stately
Old ruin I remarked: "My friends, you err—
   The truth of this is just what I expected.
This building in its time made quite a stir.
   I lived (was famous, too) when 'twas erected.
   The names here first inscribed were much respected.
This is the Hall of Fame, or I'm a stork,
And this goat-pasture once was called New York."

CONSOLATION

Little's the good to sit and grieve
Because the serpent tempted Eve.
Better to wipe your eyes and take
A club and go out and kill a snake.

But if you prefer, as I suspect,
To philosophize, why, then, reflect:
If the cunning rascal upon the limb
Hadn't tempted her she'd have tempted him.

PHILOSOPHER BIMM

Republicans think Jonas Bimm
    A Democrat gone mad,
And Democrats consider him
    Republican and bad.

The Lout reviles him as a Dude
    And gives it him right hot;
The Dude condemns his crassitude
    And calls him *sans-culottes*.

Derided as an Anglophile
    By Anglophobes, forsooth,
As Anglophobe he feels, the while,
    The Anglophilic tooth.

The Churchman calls him Atheist;
    The Atheists, rough-shod,
Have ridden o'er him long and hissed:
    "The wretch believes in God!"

The Saints whom clergymen we call
    Would kill him if they could;
The Sinners (scientists and all)
    Complain that he is good.

All men deplore the difference
    Between themselves and him,
And all devise expedients
    For paining Jonas Bimm.

I too, with wild demoniac glee,
    Would put out both his eyes;
For Mr. Bimm appears to me
    Insufferably wise!

ART

For Gladstone's portrait five thousand pounds
    Were paid, 'tis said, to Sir John Millais.
I cannot help thinking that such fine pay
Transcended reason's uttermost bounds.

For it seems to me uncommonly queer
    That a painted British statesman's price
    Exceeds the established value thrice
Of a living statesman over here.

GENESIS

God said: "Let there be Man," and from the clay
Adam came forth and, thoughtful, walked away.
The matrix whence his body was obtained,
An empty, man-shaped cavity, remained
All unregarded from that early time
Till in a recent storm it filled with slime.
Now Satan, envying the Master's power
To make the meat himself could but devour,
Strolled to the place and, standing by the pool,
Exerted all his will to make a fool.
A miracle!—from out that ancient hole
Rose Doxey, lacking nothing but a soul.

"To give him that I've not the power divine,"
Said Satan, sadly, "but I'll lend him mine."
He breathed it into him, a vapor black,
And to this day has never got it back.

THE BIRTH OF VIRTUE

When, long ago, the young world circling flew
Through wider reaches of a richer blue,
New-eyed, the men and maids saw, manifest,
The thoughts untold in one another's breast—
Each wish displayed, and every passion learned;
A look revealed them as a look discerned.
But sating Time with clouds o'ercast their eyes;
Desire was hidden, and the lips framed lies.
A goddess then, emerging from the dust,
Fair Virtue rose, the daughter of Distrust.

THE SCURRIL PRESS

Tom Jonesmith (*loquitur*): I've slept right through
The night—a rather clever thing to do.
How soundly women sleep [*looks at his wife*].
They're all alike. The sweetest thing in life
Is woman when she lies with folded tongue,
Its toil completed and its day-song sung.
[*Thump!*] That's the morning paper. What a bore
That it should be delivered at the door.
There ought to be some expeditious way
To get it *to* one. By this long delay
The fizz gets off the news [*a rap is heard*].
That's Jane, the housemaid; she's an early bird;
She's brought it to the bedroom door, good soul.
[*Gets up and takes it in.*] Upon the whole,
The system's not so bad a one. What's here?
Gad! if they've not got after—listen, dear.

[*To sleeping wife*]—young Gastrotheos. Well,
If Freedom shrieked when Kosciusko fell
She'll shriek again—with laughter—seeing how
They treated Gast. with her. Yet I'll allow
'Tis right if he goes dining at The Pup
With Mrs. Thing.
               WIFE [*briskly, waking up*]:
With her? The hussy! Yes, it serves him right.
    JONESMITH [*continuing to "seek the light"*]:
What's this about old Impycu? That's good!
Grip—that's the funny man—says Impy should
Be used as a decoy in shooting tramps.
I knew old Impy when he had the "stamps"
To buy us all out, and he wasn't then
So bad a chap to have about. Grip's pen
Is just a tickler!—and the world, no doubt,
Is better with it than it was without.
What? thirteen ladies—Jumping Jove! we know
Them nearly all!—who gamble at a low
And very shocking game of cards called "draw"!
O cracky, how they'll squirm! ha-ha! haw-haw!
Let's see what else [*wife snores*]. Well, I'll be blest!
A woman doesn't understand a jest.
Hello! What, what? the scurvy wretch proceeds
To take a fling at *me,* condemn him! [*reads*]:
Tom Jonesmith—my name's Thomas, vulgar cad!—
Of the new Shavings Bank—the man's gone mad!
That's libelous; I'll have him up for that—
Has had his corns cut. Devil take the rat!
What business is't of his, I'd like to know?
He didn't have to cut them. Gods! what low
And scurril things our papers have become!
You skim their contents and you get but scum.
Here, Mary [*waking wife*], I've been attacked
In this vile sheet. By Jove, it is a fact!
       WIFE [*reading it*]: How wicked! Who do you
Suppose 'twas wrote it?
                 JONESMITH: Who? why, who
But Grip, the so-called funny-man—he wrote
Me up because I'd not discount his note.

[Blushes like sunset at the hideous lie—
He'll think of one that's better by and by;
Throws down the paper on the floor, and treads
A merry measure on it; kicks the shreds
And patches all about the room, and still
Performs his jig with unabated will.]
    WIFE [*warbling sweetly, like an Elfland horn*]:
Dear, do be careful of that second corn.

ONE OF THE UNFAIR SEX

She stood at the ticket-seller's
    Serenely removing her glove,
While hundreds of strugglers and yellers,
    And some that were good at a shove,
      Were clustered behind her like bats in
      a cave and dissembling their love.

At night she still stood at that window
    Endeavoring her money to reach;
The crowds in her rear, how they sinned—O,
    How dreadfully sinned in their speech!
      Ten miles and a fraction extended their
      line, the historians teach.

She stands there to-day—legislation
    Has failed to remove her. The trains
No longer pull up at that station;
    And over the ghastly remains
      Of the army that waited and died of old
      age fall the snows and the rains.

THE LORD'S PRAYER ON A COIN

Upon this quarter-eagle's leveled face,
The Lord's Prayer, legibly inscribed, I trace.

"Our Father which"—the pronoun there is funny,
And shows the scribe to have addressed the money—
"Which art in Heaven"—an error this, no doubt:
The preposition should be stricken out.
Needless to quote; I only have designed
To praise the frankness of the pious mind
Which thought it natural and right to join,
With rare significancy, prayer and coin.

POLITICAL ECONOMY

"I beg you to note," said a Man to a Goose,
As he plucked from her bosom the plumage all loose,
"That pillows and cushions of feathers, and beds
As warm as maids' hearts and as soft as their heads,
Increase of life's comforts the general sum—
Which raises the standard of living." "Come, come,"
The Goose said impatiently, "tell me or cease,
How that is of any advantage to geese."
"What, what!" said the man—"you are very obtuse!
Consumption no profit to those who produce?
No good to accrue to Supply from a grand
Progressive expansion, all around, of Demand?
Luxurious habits no benefit bring
To those who purvey the luxurious thing?
Consider, I pray you, my friend, how the growth
Of luxury promises—" "Promises," quoth
The sufferer, "what?—to what course is it pledged?
To pay me for being so often defledged?"
"Accustomed"—this notion the plucker expressed
As he ripped out a handful of down from her breast—
"To one kind of luxury, people soon yearn
For others and ever for others in turn.
The man who to-night on your feathers will rest,
His mutton or bacon or beef to digest,
His hunger to-morrow will wish to assuage
With goose and a dressing of onions and sage."

INCURABLE

From pride, guile, hate, greed, melancholy—
From any kind of vice, or folly,
Bias, propensity or passion
That is in prevalence and fashion,
Save one, the sufferer or lover
May, by the grace of God, recover.
Alone that spiritual tetter,
The zeal to make creation better,
Glows still immedicably warmer.
Who knows of a reformed reformer?

PEACE

When lion and lamb have together lain down
  Spectators cry out, all in chorus:
"The lamb doesn't shrink nor the lion frown—
  A miracle's working before us!"

But 'tis patent why Hot-head his wrath holds in,
  And Faint-heart her terror and loathing;
For the one's but an ass in a lion's skin,
  The other a wolf in sheep's clothing.

THANKSGIVING

The Superintendent of an Almshouse. A Pauper.

SUPERINTENDENT:

So *you're* unthankful—you'll not eat the bird?
You sit about the place all day and gird.
I understand you'll not attend the ball
That's to be given to-night in Pauper Hall.

PAUPER:

Why, that is true, precisely as you've heard:
I have no teeth and I will eat no bird.

SUPERINTENDENT:

Ah! see how good is Providence. Because
Of teeth He has denuded both your jaws
The fowl's made tender; you can overcome it
By suction; or at least—well, you can gum it,
Confirming thus the dictum of the preachers
That Providence is good to all His creatures—
Turkeys excepted. Come, ungrateful friend,
If our Thanksgiving dinner you'll attend
You shall say grace—ask God to bless at least
The soft and liquid portions of the feast.

PAUPER:

Without those teeth my speech is rather thick—
He'll hardly understand Gum Arabic.
No, I'll not dine to-day. As to the ball,
'Tis known to you that I've no legs at all.
I had the gout—hereditary; so,
As it could not be cornered in my toe
They cut my legs off in the fond belief
That shortening me would make my anguish brief.
Lacking my legs I could not prosecute
With any good advantage a pursuit;
And so, because my father chose to court
Heaven's favor with his ortolans and port
(Thanksgiving every day!) the Lord supplied
Saws for my legs, an almshouse for my pride
And, once a year, a bird for my inside.
No, I'll not dance—my light fantastic toe
Took to its heels some twenty years ago.
Some small repairs would be required for putting
My body on a saltatory footing.

[*Sings:*]

O the legless man's an unhappy chap—
 Tum-hi, tum-hi, tum-he o'haddy.

The favors o' fortune fall not in his lap—
Tum-hi, tum-heedle-do hum.
The plums of office avoid his plate
No matter how much he may stump the State—
Tum-hi, ho-heeee.
The grass grows never beneath his feet,
But he cannot hope to make both ends meet—
Tum-hi.
With a gleeless eye and a somber heart,
He plays the rôle of his mortal part:
Wholly himself he can never be.
O, a soleless corporation is he!
  Tum.

  SUPERINTENDENT:
The chapel bell is calling, thankless friend,
Balls you may not, but church you *shall,* attend.
Some recognition cannot be denied
To the great mercy that has turned aside
The sword of death from us and let it fall
Upon the people's necks in Montreal;
That spared our city, steeple, roof and dome,
And drowned the Texans out of house and home;
Blessed all our continent with peace, to flood
The Balkan with a cataclysm of blood.
Compared with blessings of so high degree,
Your private woes look mighty small—to me.

RESTORED

Dull were the days and sober,
 The mountains were brown and bare,
For the season was sad October
 And a dirge was in the air.

The mated starlings flew over
 To the isles of the southern sea.
She wept for her warrior lover—
 Wept and exclaimed: "Ah me!

"Long years have I mourned my darling
    In his battle-bed at rest;
And it's O, to be a starling,
    With a mate to share my nest!"

The angels pitied her sorrow,
    Restoring her warrior's life;
And he came to her arms on the morrow
    To claim her and take her to wife.

An aged lover—a portly,
    Bald lover, a trifle too stiff,
With manners that would have been courtly,
    And would have been graceful, if—

If the angels had only restored him
    Without the additional years
That had passed since the enemy bored him
    To death with their long, sharp spears.

As it was, he bored her, and she rambled
    Away with her father's young groom,
And the old lover smiled as he ambled
    Contentedly back to the tomb.

TWO SHOWS

The showman (blessing in a thousand shapes!)
Parades a "School of Educated Apes!"
Small education's needed, I opine,
Or native wit, to make a monkey shine.
The brute exhibited has naught to do
But ape the larger apes that come to view—
The hoodlum with his horrible grimace,
Long upper lip and furtive, shuffling pace,
Significant reminders of the time
When hunters, not policemen, made him climb;
The lady loafer with her draggling "trail,"

That free translation of an ancient tail;
The sand-lot quadrumane in hairy suit,
Whose heels are thumbs perverted by the boot;
The painted actress throwing down the gage
To elder artists of the sylvan stage,
Proving that in the time of Noah's flood
Two ape-skins held her whole profession's blood;
The critic waiting, like a hungry pup,
To write the school—perhaps to eat it—up,
As chance or luck occasion may reveal
To earn a dollar or maraud a meal.
To view the school of apes these creatures go,
Unconscious that themselves are half the show.
These, if the simian his course but trim
To copy them as they have copied him,
Will call him "educated." Of a verity
There's much to learn by studying posterity.

TWO ROGUES

Dim, grim, and silent as a ghost,
The sentry occupied his post,
To all the stirrings of the night
Alert of ear and sharp of sight.
A sudden something—sight or sound,
About, above, or underground,
He knew not where nor what—ensued,
Thrilling the sleeping solitude.
The soldier cried: "Halt! Who goes there?"
The answer came: "Death—in the air."
"Advance, Death—give the countersign,
Or perish if you cross that line!"
To change his tone Death thought it wise—
Reminded him they'd been allies
Against the Russ, the Frank, the Turk,
In many a bloody bit of work.
"In short," said he, "in every weather

We've soldiered, you and I, together."
The sentry would not let him pass.
"Go back," he growled, "you tiresome ass—
Go back and rest till the next war,
Nor kill by methods all abhor:
Miasma, famine, filth and vice,
With plagues of locusts, plagues of lice,
Foul food, foul water, and foul gases,
Rank exhalations from morasses.
If you employ such low allies
This business you will vulgarize.
Renouncing then the field of fame
To wallow in a waste of shame,
I'll prostitute my strength and lurk
About the country doing work—
These hands to labor I'll devote,
Nor cut, by Heaven, another throat!"

NOT GUILTY

"I saw your charms in another's arms,"
 Said a Grecian swain with his blood a-boil;
"And he kissed you fair as he held you there,
 A willing bird in a serpent's coil!"

The maid looked up from the cinctured cup
 Wherein she was crushing the berries red,
Pain and surprise in her honest eyes—
 "It was only one o' those gods," she said.

THE HUMORIST

"What is that, mother?"
                    "The humorist, child.
His hands are black, but his heart is mild."

"May I touch him, mother?"
                    " 'Twere needlessly done:
He is slightly touched already, my son."

"O, why does he wear such a ghastly grin?"
" 'Tis the outward sign of a joke within."

"Will he crack it, mother?"
                    "Not so, my saint;
'Tis meant for the *Saturday Livercomplaint*."

"Does he suffer, mother?"
                    "God help him, yes!—
A thousand and fifty kinds of distress."

"What makes him sweat so?"
                    "The demons that lurk
In the fear of having to go to work."

"Why doesn't he end, then, his life with a rope?"
"Abolition of Hell has deprived him of hope."

DISCRETION

SHE:

I'm told that men have sometimes got
    Too confidential, and
Have said to one another what
    They—well, you understand.
I hope I don't offend you, sweet,
But are you sure that you're discreet?

HE:

'Tis true, sometimes my friends in wine
    Their conquests do recall,
But none can truly say that mine
    Are known to him at all.

I never, never talk you o'er—
In truth, I never get the floor.

TO A PROFESSIONAL EULOGIST

Newman, in you two parasites combine:
As tapeworm and as graveworm too you shine.
When on the virtues of the quick you've dwelt,
The pride of residence was all you felt
(What vain vulgarian the wish ne'er knew
To paint his lodging a flamboyant hue?)
And when the praises of the dead you've sung,
'Twas appetite, not truth, inspired your tongue;
As ill-bred men when warming to their wine
Boast of its merit though it be but brine.
Not gratitude incites your song, nor should—
Even Charity would shun you if she could.
You share, 'tis true, the rich man's daily dole,
But what you get you take by way of toll.
Vain to resist you—vermifuge alone
Has power to push you from your robber throne.
When to escape you he's compelled to die,
Hey! presto!—in the twinkling of an eye
You vanish as a tapeworm, reappear
As graveworm and resume your curst career.
As host no more, to satisfy your need
He serves as dinner your unaltered greed.
O thrifty sycophant to wealth and fame,
Son of servility and priest of shame,
While naught your mad ambition can abate
To lick the spittle of the rich and great;
While still like smoke your eulogies arise
To soot your heroes and inflame our eyes;
While still like smoke your eulogies arise
Down Aaron's beard, you smear each famous man,
I cannot choose but think it very odd
It ne'er occurs to you to fawn on God.

ELECTION DAY

Despots effete upon tottering thrones
Unsteadily poised upon dead men's bones,
Walk up! walk up! the circus is free,
And this wonderful spectacle you shall see:
Millions of voters who mostly are fools,
Demagogues' dupes and candidates' tools—
Armies of uniformed mountebanks,
And braying disciples of brainless cranks.
Many a week they've bellowed like beeves,
Bitterly blackguarding, lying like thieves,
Libeling freely the quick and the dead
And painting the New Jerusalem red.
Tyrants monarchical—emperors, kings,
Princes and nobles and all such things—
Noblemen, gentlemen, step this way:
There's nothing, the Devil excepted, to pay,
And the freaks and curios here to be seen
Are very uncommonly grand and serene.

No more with vivacity they debate,
Nor cheerfully crack the dissenting pate;
No longer, the dull understanding to aid,
The stomach accepts the instructive blade,
Nor the stubborn heart learns what is what
From a revelation of rabbit-shot;
And vilification's flames—behold!
Burn with a bickering faint and cold.

Magnificent spectacle!—every tongue
Suddenly civil that yesterday rung
(Like the clapper beating a brazen bell)
Each fair reputation's eternal knell;
Hands no longer delivering blows,
And noses, for counting, arrayed in rows.

Walk up, gentlemen—nothing to pay—
The Devil goes back to Hell to-day.

THE WISE AND GOOD

"O father, I saw at the church as I passed
The populace gathered in numbers so vast
That they couldn't get in; and their voices were low,
And they looked as if suffering terrible woe."

" 'Twas the funeral, child, of a gentleman dead
For whom the great heart of humanity bled."

"What made it bleed, father, for every day
Somebody, somewhere, passes away?
Do the newspaper men print a column or more
Of every person whose troubles are o'er?"

"O, no; they could never do that—and indeed,
Though printers might print it, no reader would read.
To the sepulcher all, soon or late, must be borne,
But 'tis only the Wise and Good that we mourn."

"That's right, father dear, but how can our eyes
Distinguish in dead men the Good and the Wise?"

"That's easy enough to the stupidest mind:
They're poor, and in dying leave nothing behind."

"Seest thou in mine eye, father, anything green?
And takest thy son for a gaping marine?
Go tell thy fine tale of the Wise and the Good
Who are poor, yet lamented, to babes in the wood."

And that horrible youth as I hastened away
Was building a wink that affronted the day.

A DILEMMA

Filled with a zeal to serve my fellow men,
    For years I criticized their prose and verses:
Pointed out all their blunders of the pen,
Their shallowness of thought and feeling; then
    Damned them up hill and down with hearty curses!

They said: "That's all that he can do—just sneer,
    And pull to pieces and be analytic.
Why doesn't he himself, eschewing fear,
Publish a book or two, and so appear
    As one who has the right to be a critic?

"Let him who knows it all forbear to tell
    How little others know, but *show* his learning."
And then they added: "Who has written well
May censure freely"—quoting Pope.   I fell
    Into the trap and books began out-turning,—

Books by the score—fine prose and poems fair,
    And not a book of them but was a terror,
They were so great and perfect; though I swear
I tried right hard to work in, here and there,
    (My nature still forbade) a fault or error.

'Tis true, some wretches, whom I'd scratched, no doubt,
    Professed to find—but that's a trifling matter.
Now, when the flood of noble books was out
I raised o'er all that land a joyous shout
    Till I was thought as mad as any hatter!

(Why hatters all are mad, I cannot say.
    'Twere wrong in their affliction to revile 'em,
But truly, you'll confess 'tis very sad
We wear the ugly things they make. Begad,
    They'd be less mischievous in an asylum!)

Consistency, thou art a—well, you're *paste!*
    When next I felt my demon in possession,

And made the field of authorship a waste,
All said of me: "What execrable taste,
  To rail at others of his own profession!"

Good Lord! where do the critic's rights begin
  Who has of literature some clear-cut notion,
And hears a voice from Heaven say: "Pitch in"?
He finds himself—alas, poor son of sin—
  Between the devil and the deep blue ocean!

METEMPSYCHOSIS

Once with Christ he entered Salem,
Once in Moab bullied Balaam,
Once by Apuleius staged
He the pious much enraged,
And, again, his head, as beaver,
Topped the neck of Nick the Weaver.
Omar saw him (minus tether—
Free and wanton as the weather:
Knowing naught of bit nor spur)
Stamping over Bahram-Gur.
Now, as Altgeld, see him joy
As Governor of Illinois!

THE SAINT AND THE MONK

Saint Peter at the gate of Heaven displayed
The tools and terrors of his awful trade;
The key, the frown as pitiless as night,
That slays intending trespassers at sight,
And, at his side in easy reach, the curled
Interrogation points all ready to be hurled.

Straight up the shining cloudway (it so chanced
No others were about) a soul advanced—

A fat, orbicular and jolly soul
With laughter-lines upon each rosy jowl—
A monk so prepossessing that the saint
Admired him, breathless until weak and faint,
Forgot his frown and all his questions too,
Foregoing even the customary "Who?"—
Threw wide the gate and with a friendly grin
Said: " 'Tis a very humble home, but pray walk in."

The soul smiled pleasantly. "Excuse me, please—
Who's in there?" By insensible degrees
This impudence dispelled the saint's esteem,
As dawning consciousness dispels a dream.
The frown began to blacken on his brow,
His hand to reach for "Whence?" and "Why?"
        and "How?"
"O, no offense, I hope," the soul explained;
"I'm rather—well, particular. I've strained
A point in coming here at all; 'tis said
That Susan Anthony (I hear she's dead
At last) and all her followers are here.
As company, they'd be—confess it—rather queer."

The saint replied, his rising anger past:
"What can I do?—the law is hard-and-fast,
Albeit unwritten and on earth unknown—
An oral order issued from the Throne:
By but one sin has Woman e'er incurred
God's wrath. To accuse Them Loud of that would be
        absurd."

That friar sighed, but, calling up a smile,
Said, slowly turning on his heel the while:
"Farewell, my friend.   Put up the chain and bar—
I'm going, so please you, where the pretty women are."
1895.

IN HIGH LIFE

Sir Impycu Lacquit, from over the sea,
Has led to the altar Miss Bloatie Bondee.
The wedding took place at the Church of St. Blare;
The fashion, the rank, and the wealth were all there.
No person was absent of all that one meets:
Lord Mammon himself bowed them into their seats,
While good Sir John Satan attended the door,
And Sexton Beëlzebub managed the floor,
Respectfully keeping each dog on its rug—
Preserving the peace between poodle and pug.
Twelve bridesmaids escorted the bride up the aisle,
To blush in her blush and to smile in her smile;
Twelve groomsmen supported the eminent groom,
To scowl in his scowl and to gloom in his gloom.
The rites were performed by the hand and the lip
Of his Grace the Diocesan, Osculo Grip
Assisted by three able-bodied divines;
He prayed and they grunted, he read, they made signs.
Such fashion, such beauty, such gowning, such grace
Were ne'er before seen in that heavenly place!
That night, full of gin and patrician pride,
Sir Impycu blackened the eyes of his bride.

THE GENESIS OF EMBARRASSMENT

When Adam first saw Eve he said:
"O lovely creature, share my bed."
Before consenting, she her gaze
Fixed on the greensward to appraise,
As well as vision could avouch,
The value of the proffered couch.
And seeing that the grass was green
And soft and scrupulously clean;
Observing that the flow'rs were rare
Varieties, and some were fair,
The posts of precious woods, and each

Bore luscious fruit in easy reach,
And all things suited well her worth,
She raised her angel eyes from earth
To his and, blushing to confess,
Murmured: "I love you, Adam—yes."
Since then her daughters, it is said,
Look always down when asked to wed.

BEREAVEMENT

A Countess (so they tell the tale)
Who dwelt of old in Arno's vale,
Where ladies, even of high degree,
Know more of love than of A, B, C,
Came once with a prodigious bribe
Unto the learned village scribe,
That most discreet and honest man
Who wrote for all the lover clan,
Nor e'er a secret had betrayed
Save when inadequately paid.
"Write me," she sobbed—"I pray thee do—
A book about the Prince di Giu—
A book of poetry in praise
Of all his works and all his ways;
The godlike grace of his address,
His more than woman's tenderness,
His courage stern and lack of guile,
The loves that wantoned in his smile.
So great he was, so rich and kind,
I'll not within a fortnight find
His equal as a lover. O,
My God! I shall be drowned in woe!"
"What! Prince di Giu is dead?" exclaimed
The honest man for letters famed,
The while he pocketed her gold;
"Of what?—if I may be so bold."
Fresh storms of tears the lady shed:
"I stabbed him fifty times," she said.

DETECTED

In Congress once great Mowther shone,
  Debating weighty matters;
Now into an asylum thrown,
  He vacuously chatters.

If in that legislative hall
  His wisdom still he'd vented,
It never had been known at all
  That Mowther was demented.

THE KING OF BORES

Abundant bores afflict this world, and some
  Are bores of magnitude that come and—no,
  They're always coming, but they never go—
Like funeral pageants, as they drone and hum
Their lurid nonsense like a muffled drum,
  Or bagpipe's dread, unnecessary flow.
  But one superb tormenter I can show—
Prince Fiddlefaddle, Duc de Feefawfum.
He the johndonkey is who, when I pen
  Amorous verses in an idle mood
    To nobody, or of her, reads them through
And, smirking, says he knows the lady; then
  Calls me sly dog. I wish he understood
    This tender sonnet's application too.

HISTORY

What wrecked the Roman power? One says vice,
Another indolence, another dice.
Emascle says polygamy. "Not so,"

Says Impycu—" 'twas luxury and show."
The parson, lifting up a brow of brass,
Swears superstition gave the *coup de grâce.*
Great Allison, the statesman-chap, affirms
'Twas lack of coin (croaks Medico: " 'Twas worms!")—
And John P. Jones the swift suggestion collars,
Averring the no coins were silver dollars.
Thus, through the ages, each presuming quack
Turns the poor corpse upon its rotten back,
Holds a new "autopsy" and finds that death
Resulted partly from the want of breath,
But chiefly from some visitation sad
That points his argument to serve his fad.
They're all in error—never human mind
The cause of the disaster has divined.
What slew the Roman power? Well, provided
You'll keep the secret, I will tell you. I did.

AN APOLOGUE

A traveler observed one day
A loaded fruit-tree by the way,
And reining in his horse exclaimed:
"The man is greatly to be blamed
Who, careless of good morals, leaves
Temptation in the way of thieves.
Now lest some villain pass this way
And by this fruit be led astray
To bag it, I will kindly pack
It snugly in my saddle-sack."
He did so; then that Salt o' the Earth
Rode on, rejoicing in his worth.

DIES IRAE

A recent republication of the late Gen. John A. Dix's disappointing translation of this famous medieval hymn, together with some researches into its history, which I happened to be making at the time, induces me to undertake a translation myself. It may seem presumption in me to attempt that which so many eminent scholars of so many generations have attempted before me; but failure of others encourages me to hope that success, being still unachieved, is still achievable. The fault of many translations, from Lord Macaulay's to that of Gen. Dix, has been, I venture to think, a too strict literalness, whereby the delicate irony and subtle humor of the immortal poem—though doubtless these admirable qualities were valued by the translators—have been sacrificed in the result. In none of the English versions that I have examined is more than a trace of the mocking spirit of insincerity pervading the whole prayer,—the cool effrontery of the suppliant in enumerating his demerits, his serenely illogical demands of salvation in spite, or rather because, of them, his meek submission to the punishment of others, and the many similarly pleasing characteristics of this amusing work being most imperfectly conveyed. By permitting myself a reasonable freedom of rendering—in many cases boldly supplying that "missing link" between the sublime and the ridiculous which the author, writing for the acute monkish apprehension of the thirteenth century, did not deem it necessary to insert—I have hoped at least partly to liberate the lurking devil of humor from his letters, letting him caper, not, certainly, as he does in the Latin, but as he probably would have done had his creator written in English. In preserving the meter and trochaic rhymes of the original, I have acted from the same reverent regard for the music, with which, in the liturgy of the Church, the verses have become inseparably wedded, that inspired Gen. Dix; seeking rather to surmount the obstacles to success by honest effort, than to avoid them by adopting an easier versification which would have deprived my version of all utility in religious service.

I must bespeak the reader's charitable consideration in respect of the first stanza, the insuperable difficulties of which seem to have been purposely contrived in order to warn off trespassers at the very boundary of the alluring domain. I have got over the inhibition—somehow—but David and the Sibyl must try to forgive me if they find themselves represented merely by the names of those conspicuous personal qualities to which they probably owed their powers of prophecy, as Samson's strength lay in his hair.

DIES IRAE

Dies iræ! dies illa!
Solvet sæclum in favilla
Teste David cum Sibylla.

Quantus tremor est futurus,
Quando Judex est venturus
Cuncta stricte discussurus.

Tuba mirum spargens sonum
Per sepulchra regionum,
Coget omnes ante thronum.

Mors stupebit, et Natura,
Quum resurget creatura
Judicanti responsura.

Liber scriptus proferetur,
In quo totum continetur,
Unde mundus judicetur.

Judex ergo quum sedebit,
Quicquid latet apparebit,
Nil inultum remanebit.

Quid sum miser tunc dicturus,
Quem patronem rogaturus,
Quum vix justus sit securus?

Rex tremendæ majestatis,
Qui salvandos salvas gratis;
Salva me, Fons pietatis.

Recordare, Jesu pie,
Quod sum causa tuæ viæ;
Ne me perdas illa die.

THE DAY OF WRATH

Day of Satan's painful duty!
Earth shall vanish, hot and sooty;
So says Virtue, so says Beauty.

Ah! what terror shall be shaping
When the Judge the truth's undraping—
Cats from every bag escaping!

Now the trumpet's invocation
Calls the dead to condemnation;
All receive an invitation.

Death and Nature now are quaking,
And the late lamented, waking,
In their breezy shrouds are shaking.

Lo! the Ledger's leaves are stirring,
And the Clerk, to them referring,
Makes it awkward for the erring.

When the Judge appears in session,
We shall all attend confession,
Loudly preaching non-suppression.

How shall I then make romances
Mitigating circumstances?
Even the just must take their chances.

King whose majesty amazes,
Save thou him who sings thy praises;
Fountain, quench my private blazes.

Pray remember, sacred Saviour,
Mine the playful hand that gave your
Death-blow. Pardon such behavior.

Quærens me sedisti lassus,
Redemisti crucem passus,
Tantus labor non sit cassus.

Juste Judex ultionis,
Donum fac remissionis
Ante diem rationis.

Ingemisco tanquam reus,
Culpa rubet vultus meus;
Supplicanti parce, Deus.

Qui Mariam absolvisti,
Et latronem exaudisti,
Mihi quoque spem dedisti.

Preces meæ non sunt dignæ,
Sed tu bonus fac benigne
Ne perenni cremer igne.

Inter oves locum præsta
Et ab hædis me sequestra,
Statuens in parte dextra.

Confutatis maledictis,
Flammis acribus addictis,
Voca me cum benedictis.

Oro supplex et acclinis,
Cor contritum quasi cinis;
Gere curam mei finis.

Lacrymosa dies illa
Qua resurget ex favilla,
Judicandus homo reus,
Huic ergo parce, Deus!

Seeking me, fatigue assailed thee,
Calvary's outlook naught availed thee;
Now 'twere cruel if I failed thee.

Righteous judge and learnèd brother,
Pray thy prejudices smother
Ere we meet to try each other.

Sighs of guilt my conscience gushes,
And my face vermilion flushes;
Spare me for my pretty blushes.

Thief and harlot, when repenting,
Thou forgavest—complimenting
Me with sign of like relenting.

If too bold is my petition
I'll receive with due submission
My dismissal—from perdition.

When thy sheep thou hast selected
From the goats, may I, respected,
Stand amongst them undetected.

When offenders are indicted,
And with trial-flames ignited,
Elsewhere I'll attend if cited.

Ashen-hearted, prone and prayerful,
When of death I see the air full,
Lest I perish too be careful.

On that day of lamentation,
When, to enjoy the conflagration,
Men come forth, O be not cruel:
Spare me, Lord—make them thy fuel.

SOMETHING IN THE PAPERS

"What's in the paper?" O, it's dev'lish dull:
There's nothing happening at all—a lull
After the war-storm. Mr. Someone's wife
Killed by her lover with, I think, a knife.
A fire on Blank Street and some babies—one,
Two, three or four, I don't remember, done
To quite a delicate and lovely brown.
A husband shot by woman of the town—
The same old story. Shipwreck somewhere south,
The crew all saved—or lost. Uncommon drouth
Makes hundreds homeless up the River Mud—
Though, come to think, I guess it was a flood.
'Tis feared some bank will burst—or else it won't;
They always burst I fancy—or they don't;
Who cares a cent?—the banker pays his coin
And takes his chances. Bullet in the groin—
But that's another item. Suicide—
Fool lost his money (serve him right) and died.
Heigh-ho! there's noth— Jerusalem! what's this?
Tom Jones has failed! My God, what an abyss
Of ruin!—owes me seven hundred, clear!
Was ever such a damned disastrous year?

THE MAN BORN BLIND

A man born blind received his sight
    By a painful operation;
And these are things he saw in the light
    Of an infant observation.

He saw a merchant, good and wise
    And greatly, too, respected,
Who looked, to those imperfect eyes,
    Like a swindler undetected.

He saw a patriot address
  A noisy public meeting.
He said: "Why, that's a calf, I guess,
  That for the teat is bleating."

A doctor stood beside a bed
  And shook his summit sadly.
"O see that foul assassin!" said
  The man that saw so badly.

He saw a lawyer pleading for
  A thief whom they'd been jailing,
And said: "That's an accomplice or
  My sight again is failing."

Upon the Bench a Justice sat,
  With nothing to restrain him;
" 'Tis strange," said the observer, "that
They ventured to unchain him."

With theologic works supplied,
  There was a solemn preacher;
"A burglar with his kit," he cried,
  "To rob a fellow creature."

A bluff old farmer next he saw
  Sell produce in a village,
And said: "What, what! is there no law
  To punish men for pillage?"

A dame, tall, fair and stately, passed,
  Who many charms united;
He thanked his stars his lot was cast
  Where sepulchers were whited.

He saw a soldier stiff and stern,
  "Full of strange oaths" and toddy,
But was unable to discern
  A wound upon his body.

Ten square leagues of rolling ground
   To one great man belonging,
Looked like one little grassy mound
   With worms beneath it thronging.

A palace's well carven stones,
   Where Dives dwelt contented,
Seemed built throughout of human bones
   With human blood cemented.

He watched the shining yellow thread
   A silk-worm was a-spinning;
"That creature's coining gold," he said,
   "To pay some girl for sinning."

His eyes were so untrained and dim,
   All politics, religions,
Arts, sciences, appeared to him
   But modes of plucking pigeons.

And as he drew his final breath,
   He thought he saw with sorrow
Some persons weeping for his death
   Who'd be all smiles to-morrow.

AGAIN

Well, I've met her again—at the Mission.
   She'd told me to see her no more;
It was not a command—a petition;
   I'd granted it once before.

Yes, granted it, hoping she'd write me,
   Repenting her virtuous freak—
Subdued myself daily and nightly
   For the better part of a week.

And then ('twas my duty to spare her
    The shame of recalling me) I
Just sought her again to prepare her
    For an everlasting good-bye.

O that evening of bliss—shall I ever
    Cease living it over?—although
She said, when 'twas ended: "You're never
    To see me again. And now go."

As we parted with kisses 'twas human
    And natural for me to smile
As I thought, "She's in love, and a woman:
    She'll send for me after a while."

But she didn't; so—well, the old Mission
    Is fine, picturesque and gray;
'Tis an excellent place for contrition—
    And sometimes she passes that way.

That's how it occurred that I met her,
    And that's all there is to tell—
Except that I'd like to forget her
    Calm way of remarking: "I'm well."

It was hardly worth while, all this keying
    My soul to such tensions and stirs
To learn that her food was agreeing
    With that little stomach of hers.

A SOCIAL CALL

Well, well, old Father Christmas, is it you,
    With your thick neck and thin pretense of virtue?
Less redness in the nose—nay, even some blue,
    Would not, I think, particularly hurt you.
When seen close to, not mounted in your car,
You look the drunkard and the pig you are.

No matter, sit you down, for I am not
  In a gray study, as you sometimes find me.
Merry? O, no, nor wish to be, God wot,
  But there's another year of pain behind me.
That's something to be thankful for: the more
There are behind, the fewer are before.

I know you, Father Christmas, for a scamp,
  But Heaven endowed me at my soul's creation
With an affinity to every tramp
  That walks the world and steals its admiration.
For admiration is, like linen left
Upon the line, got easiest by theft.

Good God! old man, just think of it! I've stood,
  With brains and honesty, some five-and-twenty
Long years as champion of all that's good,
  And taken on the mazzard thwacks a-plenty.
Yet now whose praises do the people bawl?
Those of the fellows whom I live to maul.

Why, this is odd!—the more I try to talk
  Of you, the more my tongue grows egotistic
To prattle of myself! I'll try to balk
  Its waywardness and be more altruistic.
So let us speak of others—how they sin,
And what a devil of a state they're in!

That's all I have to say. Good-bye, old man.
  Next year you possibly may find me scolding—
Or miss me altogether: Nature's plan
  Includes, as I suppose, a final folding
Of these poor empty hands. Then drop a tear
To think they'll never box another ear.

Selections from

SOME ANTE-MORTEM EPITAPHS

STEPHEN DORSEY

Flee, heedless stranger, from this spot accurst,
Where rests in Satan an offender first
In point of greatness, as in point of time,
Of new-school rascals who proclaim their crime.
Skilled with a frank loquacity to blab
The dark arcana of each mighty grab,
And famed for lying from his early youth,
He sinned secure behind a veil of truth.
Some lock their lips upon their deeds; some write
A damning record and conceal from sight;
Some, with a lust of speaking, die to quell it.
His way to keep a secret was to tell it.

REPARATION

Beneath this monument which rears its head,
A giant note of admiration—dead,
His life extinguished like a taper's flame,
John Ericsson is lying in his fame.

Behold how massive is the lofty shaft;
How fine the product of the sculptor's craft;
The gold how lavishly applied; the great
Man's statue how impressive and sedate!
Think what the cost was! It would ill become
Our modesty to specify the sum;
Suffice it that a fair per cent. we're giving
Of what we robbed him of when he was living.

A KIT

Here Ingalls, sorrowing, has laid
The tools of his infernal trade—
His pen and tongue. So sharp they grew,
And such destruction from them flew,
His hand was wounded when he wrote,
And when he spoke he cut his throat.

A TRENCHER-KNIGHT

Stranger, uncover; here you have in view
The monument of Chauncey M. Depew,
Eater and orator, the whole world round
For feats of tongue and tooth alike renowned.
Dining his way to eminence, he rowed
With knife and fork up water-ways that flowed
From lakes of favor—pulled with all his force
And found each river sweeter than the source.

Like rats, obscure beneath a kitchen floor,
Gnawing and rising till obscure no more,
He ate his way to eminence, and Fame
Inscribes in gravy his immortal name.

A trencher-knight, he, mounted on his belly,
So spurred his charger that its sides were jelly.
Grown desperate at last, it reared and threw him,
And Indigestion, overtaking, slew him.

Selections from

THE SCRAP HEAP

UNDERSTATED

"I'm sorry I married," says Upton Sinclair:
"The conjugal status is awful!—
The devil's device, a delusion and snare."
Worse, far worse than that—it is lawful!

FINANCIAL NEWS

Says Rockefeller: "Money is not tight,"
And, faith, I'm thinking that the man is right.
If it were not, at least in morals, loose
He hardly could command it for his use.

AN ENEMY TO LAW AND ORDER

A is defrauded of his land by B,
Who's driven from the premises by C.
D buys the place with coin of plundered E.
"That A's an Anarchist!" says F to G.

A LACKING FACTOR

"You acted unwisely," I cried, "as you see
By the outcome." He calmly eyed me:
"When choosing the course of my action," said he,
"I had not the outcome to guide me."

THE POLITICIAN

Let patriots manipulate
The tiller of the Ship of State;
Be mine the humble, useful toil
To work the tiller of the soil.

ELIHU ROOT

Stoop to a dirty trick or low misdeed?
    What, bend him from his moral skies to it?
No, no, not he! To serve his nature's need
    He may upon occasion rise to it.

AN ERROR

"I never have been able to determine
Just how it is that the judicial ermine
Is safely guarded from predacious vermin."
"It is not so, my friend; though in a garret
'Tis kept in camphor, and you often air it,
The vermin will get into it and wear it."

A PARTISAN'S PROTEST

O statesmen, what would you be at,
    With torches, flags and bands?
You make me first throw up my hat,
    And then my hands.

A PARADOX

"If life were not worth living," said the preacher,
" 'Twould have in suicide one pleasant feature."
"An error," said the pessimist, "you're making:
What's not worth having cannot be worth taking."

REEDIFIED

Lord of the Tempest, pray refrain
From leveling this church again.
Now in its doom, since so you've willed it,
We acquiesce: but *you'll* rebuild it.

A BULLETIN

"Lothario is very low,"
    So all the doctors tell.
Nay, nay, not so,—he will be, though,
    If ever he get well.

AN INSCRIPTION

For a Statue of Napoleon

A conqueror as provident as brave,
He robbed the cradle to supply the grave.
His reign laid quantities of human dust:
He fell upon the just and the unjust.

A CONSTRUCTOR

I saw the devil. He was working free—
A customs-house he builded by the sea.
"Why do you this?" The devil raised his head:
"Of churches I have built enough," he said.

UNEXPOUNDED

On Evidence, on Deeds, on Bills,
On Copyhold, on Loans, on Wills,
Lawyers great books indite.
The creaking of their busy quills
I never heard on Right.

COOPERATION

No more the swindler singly seeks his prey:
To hunt in couples is the modern way—
A rascal from the public to purloin,
An honest man to hide away the coin.

JUSTICE

She jilted me. I madly cried:
  "The grave at least can hold her!"
Reflecting then that if she died
  'Twould stop her growing older,
I pitilessly sheathed the knife
And sternly sentenced her to life!

CONVERSELY

There's grief in Belgrade, for no crown, it is said,
  Is found for King Peter in all of the town.
How sad that he's lacking a crown for his head!
  How sweet were he lacking a head for his crown!

PSYCHOGRAPHS

Says Gerald Massey: "When I write, a band
Of souls of the departed guides my hand."
How strange that poems cumbering our shelves,
Penned by immortal parts, have none themselves!

A LITERARY METHOD

His "Hoosier poems" Riley says he writes
  Upon an empty stomach. Heavenly Powers,
Feed him throat-full; for what the wretch indites
  Upon his empty stomach empties ours!

REBUKE

When Admonition's hand essays
    Our greed to curse,
Its lifted finger oft displays
    Our missing purse.

THE LONG FEAR

Noting the hangman's frown and the law's righteous rage,
Our murderers live in terror till they die of age.

Selections from

BLACK BEETLES
IN AMBER

MATTER FOR GRATITUDE

*Especially should we be thankful for having escaped the ravages of
the yellow scourge by which our neighbors have been so sorely afflicted.*
—Governor Stoneman's Thanksgiving Proclamation.

Be pleased, O Lord, to take a people's thanks
That Thine avenging sword has spared our ranks—
That thou hast parted from our lips the cup
And forced our neighbors' lips to drink it up.
Father of Mercies, with a heart contrite
We thank Thee that Thou goest south to smite,
And sparest San Francisco's loins, to crack
Thy lash on Hermosillo's bleeding back—
That o'er our homes Thine awful angel spread
A friendly wing, and Guaymas weeps instead.
We praise Thee, God, that Yellow Fever here
His horrid banner has not dared to rear,
Consumption's jurisdiction to contest,
Her dagger deep in every second breast!
Catarrh and Asthma and Congestive Chill
Attest Thy bounty and perform Thy will.
These native messengers obey Thy call—
They summon singly, but they summon all.

73

Not, as in Mexico's impested clime,
Can Yellow Jack commit recurring crime.
We thank Thee that Thou killest all the time.

Thy tender mercies, Father, never end:
Upon all heads Thy blessings still descend,
Though their forms vary. Here the sown seeds yield
Abundant grain that whitens all the field—
There the smit corn stands barren on the plain,
Thrift reaps but straw and Famine gleans in vain.
Here the fat priest to the contented king
Points to the harvest and the people sing—
There mothers eat their offspring. Well, at least
Thou hast provided offspring for the feast.
An earthquake here rolls harmless through the land,
And Thou art good because the chimneys stand—
There templed cities sink into the sea,
And damp survivors, shrieking as they flee,
Skip to the hills and hold a celebration
In honor of Thy wise discrimination.
O God, forgive them all, from Stoneman down,
Thy smile who construe and expound Thy frown,
And fall with saintly grace upon their knees
To render thanks when Thou dost only sneeze.

COMPETITION

The Seraphs came to Christ and said: "Behold!
The man, presumptuous and overbold,
Who boasted that his mercy could excel
Thine own, is dead and on his way to Hell."

Gravely the Savior asked: "What did he do
To make his impious assertion true?"

"He was a Governor, releasing all
The vilest felons ever held in thrall.

No other mortal, since the dawn of time,
Has ever pardoned such a mass of crime!"

Christ smiled benignly on the Seraphim:
"Yet I am victor, for I pardon *him*."

RELIGIOUS PROGRESS

*Every religion is important. When men rise above existing con-
ditions a new religion comes in, and it is better than the old one.—*
Professor Howison.

Professor dear, I think it queer
    That all these good religions
('Twixt you and me, some two or three
    Are schemes for plucking pigeons)—

I mean 'tis strange that every change
    Our poor minds to unfetter
Entails a new religion—true
    As t' other one, and better.

From each in turn the truth we learn,
    That wood or flesh or spirit
May justly boast it rules the roast
    Until we cease to fear it.

Nay, once upon a time long gone
    Man worshipped Cat and Lizard:
His God he'd find in any kind
    Of beast, from a to izzard.

When risen above his early love
    Of dirt and blood and slumber,
He pulled down these vain deities,
    And made one out of lumber.

"Far better that than even a cat,"
The Howisons all shouted;
"When God is wood religion's good!"
But one poor cynic doubted.

"A timber God—that's very odd!"
Said Progress, and invented
The simple plan to worship Man,
Who, kindly soul! consented.

But soon our eye we lift asky,
Our vows all unregarded,
And find (at least so says the priest)
The Truth—and Man's discarded.

Along our line of march recline
Dead gods devoid of feeling;
And thick about each sun-cracked lout
Dried Howisons are kneeling.

THE FALL OF MISS LARKIN

Hear me sing of Sally Larkin who, I'd have you understand,
Played accordions as well as any lady in the land;
And I've often heard it stated that her fingering was such
That Professor Schweinenhauer was enchanted with her
   touch,
And that beasts were so affected when her apparatus rang
That they dropped upon their haunches and deliriously
   sang.
This I know from testimony, though a critic, I opine,
Needs an ear that is dissimilar in some respects to mine.
She could sing, too, like a jaybird, and they say all eyes were
   wet
When Sally and the ranch-dog were performing a duet—
Which I take it is a song that has to be so loudly sung
As to overtax the strength of any single human lung.

That, at least, would seem to follow from the tale I have to
tell,
Which (I've told you how she flourished) is how Sally Larkin
fell.

One day there came to visit Sally's dad as sleek and smart
A chap as ever wandered there from any foreign part.
Though his gentle birth and breeding he did not at all
obtrude
It was somehow whispered round he was a simon-pure Dude.
Howsoe'er that may have been, it was conspicuous to see
That he was a real Gent of an uncommon high degree.
That Sally cast her tender and affectionate regards
On this exquisite creation was, of course, upon the cards;
But he didn't seem to notice, and was variously blind
To her many charms of person and the merits of her mind,
And preferred, I grieve to say it, to play poker with her dad,
And acted in a manner that in general was bad.

One evening—'t was in summer—she was holding in her lap
Her accordion, and near her stood that melancholy chap,
Leaning up against a pillar with his lip in grog imbrued,
Thinking, maybe, of that ancient land in which he was a
Dude.
Now Sally, who was melancholy too, began to hum
And elongate the accordion with a preluding thumb.
Then sighs of amorosity she painfully exhaled,
And her music apparatus sympathetically wailed.
"In the gloaming, O my darling!" rose that wild impassioned
strain,
And her eyes were fixed on his with an intensity of pain,
Till the ranch-dog from his kennel at the postern gate came
round,
And going into session strove to magnify the sound.
He lifted up his spirit till the gloaming rang and rang
With the song that to *his* darling he impetuously sang!
Then that musing youth, recalling all his soul from other
scenes,
Where his fathers all were Dudes and his mothers all
Dudines,

From his lips removed the beaker and politely, o'er the grog,
Said: "Miss Larkin, please be quiet: you will interrupt the
    dog."

AN ART CRITIC

Ira P. Rankin, you've a nasal name—
I'll sound it through "the speaking-trump of fame,"
And wondering nations, hearing from afar
The brazen twang of its resounding jar,
Shall say: "These bards are an uncommon class—
They blow their noses with a tube of brass!"

So you object to Cytherea! Do,
The picture was not painted, sir, for you!
Your mind to gratify and taste address,
The masking dove had been a dove the less.
Provincial censor! all untaught in art,
With mind indecent and indecent heart,
Do you not know—nay, why should I explain?
Instruction, argument alike were vain—
I'll show you reasons when you show me brain.

THE TRANSMIGRATIONS OF A SOUL

What! Pixley, must I hear you call the roll
Of all the vices that infest your soul?
Was't not enough that lately you did bawl
Your money-worship in the ears of all?
Still must you crack your brazen cheek to tell
That though a miser you're a sot as well?
Still must I hear how low your taste has sunk—
From getting money down to getting drunk?

Who worships money, damning all beside,
And shows his callous knees with pious pride,
Speaks with half-knowledge, for no man e'er scorns
His own possessions, be they coins or corns.
You've money, neighbor; had you gentle birth
You'd know, as now you never can, its worth.

You've money; learning is beyond your scope,
Deaf to your envy, stubborn to your hope.
But if upon your undeserving head
Science and letters had their glory shed;
If in the cavern of your skull the light
Of knowledge shone where now eternal night
Breeds the blind, poddy, vapor-fatted naughts
Of cerebration that you think are thoughts—
Black bats in cold and dismal corners hung
That squeak and gibber when you move your tongue—
You would not write, in Avarice's defense,
A senseless eulogy on lack of sense,
Nor show your eagerness to sacrifice
All noble virtues to one loathsome vice.

You've money; if you'd manners too you'd shame
To boast your weakness or your baseness name.
Appraise the things you have, but measure not
The things denied to your unhappy lot.
He values manners lighter than a cork
Who combs his beard at table with a fork.
Hare to seek sin and tortoise to forsake,
The laws of taste condemn you to the stake
To expiate, where all the world may see,
The crime of growing old disgracefully.

Distinction, learning, birth and manners, too,
All that distinguishes a man from you,
Pray damn at will: all shining virtues gain
An added luster from a rogue's disdain.
But spare the young that proselyting sin,
A toper's apotheosis of gin.
If not our young, at least our pigs may claim
Exemption from the spectacle of shame!

Are you not he who lately out of shape
Blew a brass trumpet to denounce the grape?—
Who led the brave teetotalers afield
And slew your leader underneath your shield?—
Swore that no man should drink unless he flung
Himself across your body at the bung?—
Who vowed if you'd the power you would fine
The Son of God for making water wine?

All trails to odium you tread and boast,
Yourself enamored of the dirtiest most.
One day to be a miser you aspire,
The next to wallow drunken in the mire;
The third, lo! you're a meritorious liar!
Pray, in the catalogue of all your graces
Have theft and cowardice no honored places?

Yield thee, great Satan—here's a rival name
With all thy vices and but half thy shame!
Quick to the letter of the precept, quick
To the example of the elder Nick;
With as great talent as was e'er applied
To fool a teacher and to fog a guide;
With slack allegiance and boundless greed,
To paunch the profit of a traitor deed,
He aims to make thy glory all his own,
And crowd his master from the infernal throne!

TO AN ASPIRANT

What! you a Senator?—you, Mike de Young?
Still reeking of the gutter whence you sprung?
Sir, if all Senators were such as you—
Their hands so slender and so crimson too
(Shaped to the pocket for commercial work,
For literary, fitted to the dirk)—
So black their hearts, so lily-white their livers—
The toga's touch would give a man the shivers!

HELL

The friends who stood about my bed
Looked down upon my face and said:
"God's will be done—the fellow's dead."

When from my body I was free
I straightway felt myself, ah me!
Sink downward to the life to be.

Full twenty centuries I fell,
And then alighted. "Here you dwell
For aye," a Voice cried—"this is Hell!"

A landscape lay about my feet,
Where trees were green and flowers sweet.
The climate was devoid of heat.

The sun looked down with gentle beam,
Upon the bosom of the stream,
Nor saw I any sign of steam.

The waters by the sky were tinged,
The hills with light and color fringed.
Birds warbled on the wing unsinged.

"Ah, no, this is not Hell," I cried;
"The preachers ne'er so greatly lied,
This is Earth's spirit glorified!

"Good souls do not in Hades dwell,
And, look, there's John P. Irish!" "Well,"
The Voice said, "that's what makes it Hell."

"DIED OF A ROSE"

A reporter he was, and he wrote, wrote he:
"The grave was covered as thick as could be
  With floral tributes"—which reading,

The editor man he said, he did so:
"For 'floral tributes' he's got for to go,
    For I hold the same misleading."
Then he called him in and he pointed sweet
To a blooming garden across the street,
    Inquiring: "What's them a-growing?"
The reporter chap said: "Why, where's your eyes?
Them's floral tributes!" "Arise, arise,"
    The editor said, "and be going."

A CELEBRATED CASE

Way down in the Boom Belt lived Mrs. Roselle;
A person named Petrie, he lived there as well;
But Mr. Roselle he resided away—
Sing tooral iooral iooral iay.

Once Mrs. Roselle in her room was alone:
The flesh of her flesh and the bone of her bone
Neglected the wife of his bosom to woo—
Sing tooral iooral iooral ioo.

Then Petrie, her lover, appeared at the door,
Remarking: "My dear, I don't love you no more."
"That's awfully rough," said the lady, "on me—
Sing tooral iooral iooral iee."

"Come in, Mr. Petrie," she added, "pray do:
Although you don't love me no more, I love you.
Sit down while I spray you with vitriol now—
Sing tooral iooral iooral iow."

Said Petrie, "That liquid I know won't agree
With my beauty, and then you'll no longer love me;
So spray and be"—O, what a word he did say!—
Sing tooral iooral iooral iay.

She deluged his head and continued to pour
Till his bonny blue eyes, like his love, were no more.
It was seldom he got such a hearty shampoo—
Sing tooral iooral iooral ioo.

Then Petrie he rose and said: "Mrs. Roselle,
I have an engagement and bid you farewell."
"You see," she began to explain—but not he!—
Sing tooral iooral iooral iee.

The Sheriff he came and he offered his arm,
Saying, "Sorry I am for disturbin' you, marm,
But business is business." Said she, "So they say—
Sing tooral iooral iooral iay."

The Judge on the bench he looked awfully stern;
The District Attorney began to attorn;
The witnesses lied and the lawyers—O my!—
Sing tooral iooral iooral iyi.

The chap that defended her said: "It's our claim
That he loved us no longer and told us the same.
What else than we did could we decently do?—
Sing tooral iooral iooral ioo."

The District Attorney, sarcastic, replied:
"We loved you no longer—that can't be denied.
Not having no eyes, we may dote on you now—
Sing tooral iooral iooral iow."

The prisoner wept to entoken her fears;
The sockets of Petrie were flooded with tears.
O heaven-born Sympathy, bully for you!—
Sing tooral iooral iooral ioo.

Four jurors considered the prisoner mad,
And four thought her victim uncommonly bad,
And four that the acid was "all in his eye"—
Sing rum tiddy iddity iddity hi.

THREE HIGHWAYMEN

A street contractor, t'other morn,
Walked out before the day was born.
The silver moon beyond his reach
Had prudently retired, and each
Fair golden star his clutch that feared
Trembled, grew pale, and disappeared.
The sun rose not—afraid to risk
His tempting, double-eagle disk.
Our hero—why spin out the verse?—
Two robbers robbed him of his purse,
Left him uncomfortably spread
On his own pavement, semi-dead,
And ran away exultant. He
Sang "Murder!" "Fire!" in every key,
Until politeness bade him cease
For fear of waking the police.
Then straight unto the Chief, all faint,
He made his way and his complaint:
"I met two robber-men," said he;
"We battled and—well, look at *me!*—
Sad citizen, O Chief, you see."
"How much?" asked that sententious man
"Well, sir, as nearly as I can
Compute it, though I gave them fits,
They got away—with my six bits."
"Why, damn your avaricious soul!"
The Chief said: "do you claim the whole?
You did quite well to get, begad,
Within six bits of all they had!"

UNARMED

Saint Peter sat at the jasper gate,
When Senator White arrived in state,

"Admit me." "With pleasure," Peter said,
Pleased to observe that the man was dead;

"That's what I am here for. Kindly show
Your ticket, my lord, and in you go."

White stared in blank surprise. Said he:
"I *run* this place—just turn that key."

"Yes?" said the Saint; the Senator heard
With pain the inflection of that word.

But, mastering his emotion, he
Remarked: "My friend, you're too damned free;

"I'm Stephen M., by thunder, White!"
And, "Yes?" the guardian said, with quite

The self-same irritating stress
Distinguishing his former yes.

And still demurely as a mouse
He twirled the key to that Upper House.

Then Stephen, seeing his bluster vain
Admittance to those halls to gain,

Said, neighborly: "Pray tell me, Pete,
Does any one contest my seat?"

The Saint replied: "Nay, nay, not so;
But you voted always wrong below:

"Whate'er the question, clear and high
Your voice rang: '*I*,' '*I*,' ever '*I*.'"

Now indignation fired the heart
Of that insulted immortal part.

"Die, wretch!" he cried, with blanching lip,
And made a motion to his hip,

With purpose murderous and hearty,
To draw the Democratic party!

He felt his fingers vainly slide
Upon his unappareled hide

(The dead arise from their "silent tents"
But not their late habiliments)

Then wailed—the briefest of his speeches:
"I've left it in my other breeches!"

A "SCION OF NOBILITY"

Come, sisters, weep!—our Baron dear,
   Alas! has run away.
If always we had kept him here
   He had not gone astray.

Painter and grainer it were vain
   To say he was, before;
And if he was, yet ne'er again
   He'll darken here a door.

We mourn each matrimonial plan—
   Even tradesmen join the cry:
He was so promising a man
   Whenever he did buy.

He was a fascinating lad,
   Deny it all who may;
Even "moneyed" men confess he had
   A very taking way.

So from our tables he is gone—
   Our tears descend in showers;
We loved the very fat upon
   His kidneys, for 'twas ours.

To women he was all respect,
   To duns as cold as ice;
No lady could his suit reject,
   No tailor get its price.

He raised our hope above the sky;
   Alas! alack! and O!
That one who worked it up so high
   Should play it down so low.

AN INTERPRETATION

Now Lonergan appears upon the boards,
And Truth and Error sheathe their lingual swords.
No more in wordy warfare to engage,
The commentators bow before the stage,
And bookworms, militant for ages past,
Confess their equal foolishness at last,
Re-read their Shakespeare in the newer light
And swear the meaning's obvious to sight.
For centuries the question has been hot:
Was Hamlet crazy, or was Hamlet not?
Now, Lonergan's illuminating art
Reveals the truth of the disputed "part,"
And shows to all the critics of the earth
That Hamlet was an idiot from birth!

WITH A BOOK

Words shouting, singing, smiling, frowning—
   Sense lacking.
Ah, nothing more obscure than Browning,
   Save blacking.

ON THE PLATFORM

When Dr. Bill Bartlett stepped out of the hum
   Of Mammon's distracting and wearisome strife
To stand and deliver a lecture on "Some
   Conditions of Intellectual Life,"
I cursed the offender who gave him the hall
To lecture on any conditions at all!

But he rose with a fire divine in his eye,
   Haranguing with endless abundance of breath,
Till I slept; and I dreamed of a gibbet reared high,
   And Dr. Bill Barlett was dressing for death.
And I thought in my dream: "These conditions, no doubt,
Are bad for the life he was talking about."

So I cried (pray remember this all was a dream):
   "Get down off the platform!—it isn't the kind!"
But he fell through the trap, with a jerk at the beam,
   And wiggled his toes to unburden his mind.
And, O, so bewitching the thoughts he advanced
That I clung to his ankles, attentive, entranced!

DESPERATION

My days all are wasted in vainly
   Contesting the field against Fate;
My nights with remorses insanely
   Are swarming, and spectres of hate.

"O for rest! O for peace!" I cry madly—
   "Let me fall, for I faint in the strife.
To be dead, to be dead, I'd give gladly
   All, all that I have, except life."

TO DOG

Pervading pest! Old Adam, when he saw
  Thy prime progenitor, I doubt not, swore
  And kicked the curst kioodle from the door,
Though now thy whelpage we protect by law.
In faith, thou must have been a beastly, raw,
  Uncultivated monster many score
  Immemorable centuries before
Thy rigor was by breeding made to thaw.
How racy of the soil thou must have been!—
  Indigenous and close to nature's heart!
How strong thy jaw-lock, habits how unclean,
  And what a sink of infamy thy heart!
It may be, though, thou wert created upright.
If Man (the angels' care) could fall, a pup might.

MEMORIAL DAY

The bands have played, the singers finished singing,
The flags done flapping and the bells done ringing.
Hereditary candidates have spoken;
Their tongues are silent and their hearts are broken—
Barnes, Shortridge, Salomon-in-all-his-glory,
With wounds (their mouths) no longer wide and gory—
Healed by the touch of time; for even orations
Must sometimes come to end if one have patience.
And still in spite of all the din infernal
Of every "General" and "Judge" and "Colonel,"
Our grand old heroes sleep in peace eternal!

ADAIR WELCKER, POET

The Swan of Avon died—the Swan
Of Sacramento'll soon be gone;
And when his death-song he shall coo,
Stand back, or it will kill you too.

CONTENT

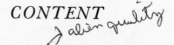
of alien quality

One day when Satan visited the earth
In order that his eyes might feed his mirth,
A loyal follower in sorrow said,
"Father of Falsehood, to our idols wed
We rear memorials in bronze and stone
To every kind of mortal greatness known;
But not in this thy realm stands anywhere
A monument or statue to declare
Thy greater glory." With the modest mien
Of violet that loves to bloom unseen,
Satan replied: "All earthly fame I shun,
Content with consciousness of work well done.
Statues to heroes! Mine the humble glory
To tell on every pedestal the story."

THE GENESIS OF CRIME

God said, "Let there be Crime," and the command
Brought Satan, leading Stoneman by the hand.
"Why, that's Stupidity, not Crime," said God—
"Bring what I ordered." Satan with a nod
Replied, "This is *one* element—when I
The *other*—Opportunity—supply
In just equivalent, the two'll affine
And in a chemical embrace combine
And Crime result; for Crime can only be
Stupiditate of Opportunity."
So leaving Stoneman (not as yet endowed
With soul) in special session on a cloud,
Nick to his sooty laboratory went,
Returning soon with t'other element.
"Here's Opportunity," he said, and put
Pen, ink and paper down at Stoneman's foot.
He seized them—Heaven was filled with fires and thunders,
And Crime was added to Creation's wonders!

RECONCILIATION

Stanford and Huntington, so long at outs,
Kissed and made up. If you have any doubts
Dismiss them, for I saw them do it, man;
And then—why, then I clutched my purse and ran.

A RATIONAL ANTHEM

My country, 'tis of thee,
Sweet land of felony,
    Of thee I sing—
Land where my fathers fried
Young witches and applied
Whips to the Quaker's hide
    And made him spring.

My knavish country, thee,
Land where the thief is free,
    Thy laws I love;
I love thy thieving bills
That tap the people's tills;
I love thy mob whose will's
    All laws above.

Let Federal employees
And rings rob all they please,
    The whole year long.
Let office-holders make
Their piles and judges rake
Our coin. For Jesus' sake,
    Let's *all* go wrong!

FIG LEAF

(*A Definition*)

An artist's trick by which the Nude's
Protected from the eyes of prudes,
Which else with their peculiar flame
Might scorch the canvas in its frame,
Or melt the bronze, or burn to lime
The marble, in a minute's time.
For sparks are sometimes seen to dance
Where falls a dame's offended glance,
And little curls of smoke to rise
From fingers veiling virgin eyes.

O prudes I know you,—once you made
Among us here a fool crusade
Against some casts from the antique,
Great, naked, natural and Greek,
Whereto you flocked, a prurient crush,
And diligently tried to blush,
Half strangled in the vain attempt
Till some one (may the wretch be hemped!)
Depressed his lordly length of ear
Your loud lubricity to hear,
Then took his chisel up and dealt
At Art a blow below the belt.
Insulted, crimson with the shame,
Her cheeks aglow, her eyes aflame,
The goddess spread her pinions bright,
Sprang, and the town was left in night!

Since then in vain the painter toils:
His canvas still repels the oils.
In vain with melancholy sighs
His burin the engraver plies;
Lines multiply beneath his hand—
Their meaning none can understand.
With stubborn clay and unsubdued,

The sculptor shapes his fancies crude,
Unable to refine the work,
And makes a god look like a Turk.
To marble grown, or metal, still
The monstrous image makes him ill,
Till, crazed with rage, the damaged lot
He breaks, or sells to Irving Scott.

COMPLIANCE

Said Rockefeller, senior, to his boy:
"Be good and you shall have eternal joy."
Said Rockefeller, junior, to his dad:
"I never do a single thing that's bad."
Said Rockefeller, senior—long gone gray
In service at the altar: "Ever pray."
And Rockefeller, junior, being bid,
Upon his knees and neighbors ever did.

THE NEW DECALOGUE

Have but one God: thy knees were sore
If bent in prayer to three or four.

Adore no images save those
The coinage of thy country shows.

Take not the Name in vain. Direct
Thy swearing unto some effect.

Thy hand from Sunday work be held—
Work not at all unless compelled.

Honor thy parents, and perchance
Their wills thy fortunes may advance.

Kill not—death liberates thy foe
From persecution's constant woe.

Kiss not thy neighbor's wife. Of course
There's no objection to divorce.

To steal were folly, for 'tis plain
In cheating there is greater gain.

Bear not false witness. Shake your head
And say that you have "heard it said."

Who stays to covet ne'er will catch
An opportunity to snatch.

YE FYGHTYNGE SEVENTH

It is the gallant Seventh—
    It fyghteth faste and free!
God wot the where it fyghteth
    I ne desyre to be.

The Gonfalon it flyeth,
    Seeming a Flayme in Sky;
The Bugel loud yblowen is,
    Which sayeth, Doe and dye!

And (O good Saints defende us
    Agaynst the Woes of Warr)
Drawn Tongues are flashing deadly
    To smyte the Foeman sore!

With divers kinds of Riddance
    The smoking Earth is wet,
And all aflowe to seaward goe
    The Torrents wide of Sweat!

The Thunder of the Captens,
    And eke the Shouting, mayketh
Such horrid Din the Soule within
    The boddy of me quayketh!

Whom fyghteth the bold Seventh?
    What haughty Power defyes?
Their Colonel 'tis they drubben sore,
    And dammen too his Eyes!

TO AN INSOLENT ATTORNEY

So, Hall McAllister, you'll not be warned—
My protest slighted, admonition scorned!
To save your scoundrel client from a cell
As loth to swallow him as he to swell
Its sum of meals insurgent (it decries
All wars intestinal with meats that rise)
You turn your scurril tongue against the press
And damn the agency you ought to bless.
Had not the press with all its hundred eyes
Discerned the wolf beneath the sheep's disguise
And raised the cry upon him, he to-day
Would lack your company, and you would lack his pay.

Talk not of "hire" and consciences for sale—
You whose profession 'tis to threaten, rail,
Calumniate and libel at the will
Of any villain who can pay the bill,—
You whose most honest dollars all were got
By saying for a fee "the thing that's not!"
To you 'tis one, to challenge or defend;
Clients are means, their money is an end.
In my profession sometimes, as in yours
Always, a payment large enough secures
A mercenary service to defend
The guilty, or the innocent to rend.
But mark the difference, nor think it slight:

We do not hold it proper, just and right;
Of selfish lies a little still we shame
And give our villainies another name.
Hypocrisy's an ugly vice, no doubt,
But blushing sinners can't get on without.
Happy the lawyer!—at his favored hands
Nor truth nor decency the world demands.
Secure in his immunity from shame,
His cheek ne'er kindles with the tell-tale flame.
His brains for sale, morality for hire,
In every land and century a licensed liar!

No doubt, McAllister, you can explain
How honorable 'tis to lie for gain,
Provided only that the jury's made
To understand that lying is your trade.
A hundred thousand volumes, broad and flat,
(The Bible not included) proving that,
Have been put forth, though still the doubt remains
If God has read them with befitting pains.
No Morrow could get justice, you'll declare,
If none who knew him foul affirmed him fair.
Ingenious man! how easy 'tis to raise
An argument to justify the course that pays!

I grant you, if you like, that men may need
The services performed for crime by greed,—
Grant that the perfect welfare of the State
Requires the aid of those who in debate
As mercenaries lost in early youth
The fine distinction between lie and truth,—
Who cheat in argument and set a snare
To take the feet of Justice unaware,—
Who serve with livelier zeal when rogues assist
With perjury, embracery (the list
Is long to quote) than when an honest soul,
Scorning to plot, conspire, intrigue, cajole,
Reminds them (their astonishment how great!)
He'd rather suffer wrong than perpetrate.
I grant, in short, 'tis better all around

That ambidextrous consciences abound
In courts of law to do the dirty work
That self-respecting scavengers would shirk.
What then? Who serves however clean a plan
By doing dirty work, he is a dirty man!

THE FARMERS' PRAYER

O Lord, incline Thine ear unto our prayer
    And preachers' intercession:
This strange discrimination is unfair—
    That's our impression.

Our neighbors all about have copious rains
    That fall on them like manna.
Send *us* the showers, Lord, and parch the plains
    Of Indiana.

Upon the just and unjust, sayest Thou,
    Thou'lt sprinkle without favor.
The sin of promise-breaking, all allow,
    Could not be graver.

We're just, and still our whistles are not wet,
    And still 'tis growing hotter;
While every scamp in Michigan can get
    His fill of water.

We ask but justice: treat us not with scorn;
    Our comfort make less chilly;
And those who pray for an advance in corn—
    O smite them silly!

Let corn be plentiful, and cheap: our hops
    Look well without a shower;
We've sold our wheat: that profitable crop's
    Beyond Thy power.

A MILITARY INCIDENT

Dawn heralded the coming sun—
For Douglas was computing
The minute—and the sunrise gun
Was manned for his saluting.

The gunner at that firearm stood,
The which he slowly loaded,
When, bang!—I know not how it could,
But sure the charge exploded!

Yes, to that veteran's surprise
The gun went off sublimely,
And both his busy arms likewise
Went off with it, untimely.

Then said that gunner to his mate
(He was from Ballyshannon):
"Bedad, the sun's a minute late,
Accardin' to this cannon!"

THE LEADER OF THE MINORITY

He tolls them along through the wilderness dire,
Ever in sight—
A clod by day and a pillar of fire-
Water by night.

GEORGE C. PERKINS

Running for Senator with clumsy pace,
He stooped so low to win the foremost place
That Fortune, tempted by a mark so droll,
Sprang in and kicked him to the winning pole.

ARBOR DAY

Hasten, children, black and white—
Celebrate the yearly rite.
Every pupil plant a tree:
It will grow some day to be
Big and strong enough to bear
A School Director hanging there.

CALIFORNIAN SUMMER PICTURES

THE FOOT-HILL RESORT

Assembled in the parlor
  Of the place of last resort,
The smiler and the snarler
  And the guests of every sort—
    The elocution chap
    With rhetoric on tap;
  The mimic and the funny dog;
  The social sponge; the money-hog;
    Vulgarian and dude;
    And the prude;
  The adiposing dame
  With pimply face aflame:
  The kitten-playful virgin
    Of a half-a-hundred years;
  The solemn-staring sturgeon
    Of a firm of auctioneers;
  The widower flirtatious;
  The widow all too gracious;
The man with a proboscis and a sepulcher beneath.
One assassin picks his banjo, and another one his teeth.

THE IN-COMING CLIMATE

Now o' nights the ocean breeze
  Makes the patient flinch,

For that zephyr bears a sneeze
In every cubic inch.
Lo! the admiring population
Chorusing in sternutation
A catarrhal acclamation!

A LONG-FELT WANT

Dimly apparent, through the gloom
Of Market-street's opaque simoom,
A queue of people, parti-sexed,
Awaiting the command of "Next!"
A sidewalk booth, a dingy sign:
"Teeth dusted nice—five cents a shine."

TO THE HAPPY HUNTING GROUNDS

Wide windy reaches of high stubble field;
A long gray road, bordered with dusty pines;
A wagon moving in a "cloud by day";
Two city sportsmen with a dove between,
Breast-high upon a fence and fast asleep—
A solitary dove, the only dove
In twenty counties, and it sick, or else
It were not there. Two guns that fire as one,
With thunder simultaneous and loud;
Two shattered human wrecks of blood and bone!
And later, in the gloaming, comes a man—
The worthy local coroner is he,
Renowned all thereabout, and popular
With many a remain. All tenderly
Compiling in a game-bag the remains,
He glides into the gloom and fades from sight.
The dove, cured of its ailment by the shock,
Has flown, meantime, on pinions strong and fleet,
To die of age in some far foreign land.

SLANDER

FITCH:

"All vices you've exhausted, friend;
  So all the papers say."

PICKERING:

"Ah, what vile calumnies are penned!—
  'Tis just the other way."

PRIVATION

With her grief the widow was so engrossed
  As she rode at the hearse's rear,
That I really think the dead man's ghost
  Must have shed the ghost of a tear.

She murmured and moaned and wiped her eyes
  And blew her pale nose for relief,
Then started and cried, as in pained surprise,
  "I've forgotten my handkerchief!

"O, what shall I do when we get to the grave
  And the coffin is put in the ground?
I know I shall weep, for I cannot be brave
  With those staring people all round."

"Be calm," said one; "there is nothing forgot,
  For your handkerchief you bring—
You are holding it—see." Said the widow: "What!
  This pokey old linen thing?"

IN WARNING

They tell us, dear Kipling, you're coming to shoot
  In the hills of the wide, wild West.

There's a lot of cost and a risk to boot—
   I don't at all think it is best,
   And hope it is only a jest.

For, Rudyard, although you're a terrible swell
   You're not in high favor out here;
For you said San Francisco was meaner than—well,
   You said it was very small beer
   And Chicago uncommonly queer.

You put your legs under our tables, you did,
   You dined at the Jollidog Club;
And when of your hunger you well were rid
   (And your manners too) like a cub
   You snarled at the speeches and grub.

You said—I don't know the one half that you said,
   But I know you pretended to meet
Some folk that existed not out of your head
   Or an English comical sheet.
   And you vilified Kearny street!

Our statesmen apparently didn't get far
   In the favor of one so too,
Too utterly fine. Nor the plump cigar
   Nor the shiny hat could woo
   The sweet and beautiful You.

But hardest of all our hearts you wrung
   With assorted pangs and woes
When you said you could speak the English tongue,
   But not the American nose.
   And you damned our orators' o's!

For all of this and for all of that
   You'd better abate your flame,
And remain where pheasants are tame and fat
   And the sportsman takes his aim,
   As a general thing, at the game.

Out here when we go to shoot, perhaps
   Nor beast nor bird we see;
So we just let go at the Britisher chaps
   Who have made remarks too free,
   And the same surcease to be.

A CREDITABLE COLLISION

   There was once a brave collision
     In Imaginary Bay,
   When a steamer with precision
     Clove its comfortable way
Through another, which had hospitably stood
To receive it, as a civil steamer should.

   Then the people on the latter
     Said they didn't understand,
   But they thought they'd better scatter
     To the most adjacent land;
And the people on the former said: "That's so—
You will find it sixty fathoms down below."

   Then the skipper of the vessel
     Which was sinking in the brine
   Said to t'other one: "I guess I'll
     Trouble you to drop a line."
"Well, just give me your address," was the reply,
"I am busy but I'll write you by-and-by."

   Then the carpenter whose function
     Was to mend the leaky boat
   Said: "So wide is our disjunction
     That we cannot longer float.
See the rats already leave us!" And so he
Up and hove his kit among them in the sea.

   Though these incidents are cheerful
     For a landsman to relate,

Yet the passengers were fearful
Of a melancholy fate;
For their knowledge was imperfect of the way
That the fishes have of breathing in the bay.

Some of them, who were accounted
Quite unmannerly and rude,
On the floating steamer mounted,
Saying: "Hope we don't intrude."
But the others, with politeness rare and fine,
Said their tickets were not good upon that line.

But the skipper of the wetter
Ship, the pilot and the mate—
Nothing ever yet was better
Than the way they met their fate;
For the perils that beset them in their climb
They encountered with alacrity sublime.

When the troubles all were ended
And the living safe in port
Invitation was extended
For them all to come to court.
Where the officers (they afterward explained)
Were with deferential kindness entertained.

Twenty Consuls, ten Inspectors,
Thirty Coroners were there,
Eighty-seven skilled objectors
And a Notary to swear;
And before that court the sailor-people sighed
And expounded how the passengers had lied.

The unanimous decision
Of that high and mighty court
Was "spontaneous collision"—
(I am quoting the report)
And the skippers were commended who had fed
To the lobsters each a bellyful of dead.

THE MUMMERY

THE BIRTH OF THE RAIL

DRAMATIS PERSONAE

LELAND THE KID ....*a Road Agent*
COWBOY CHARLEY ....*Same Line of Business*
HAPPY HUNTY ....*Ditto in All Ways*
SOOTYMUG ....*a Devil*

Scene—The Dutch Flat Stage Road, at 12 P.M., on a Night of 1864.

COWBOY CHARLEY:

I fear the coach will not come by to-night.
Already it is past the hour, and yet
My ears have reached no sound of wheels; no note
Melodious, of long, luxurious oaths
Betokens the traditional dispute
(Unsettled from the dawn of time) between
The driver and off wheeler; no clear chant
Nor carol of Wells Fargo's messenger
Unbosoming his soul upon the air—
Singing his prowess to the tenderfoot,
And how at divers times in sundry ways
He strewed the roadside with our carcasses.
Clearly, the stage-coach will not pass to-night.

LELAND THE KID:

I now remember that but yesterday
I saw three ugly looking fellows start
From Colfax with a gun apiece, and they
Did seem on business of importance bent,
Furtively casting all their eyes about
And covering their tracks with all the care
That business men do use. I think perhaps
They were Directors of that rival line,
The great Pacific Mail. If so, they have
Indubitably taken in that coach,
And we are overreached. Three times before
This thing has happened, and if once again
These outside operators dare to cut
Our rates of profit I shall quit the road
And take my money out of this concern.
When robbery no longer pays expense
It loses then its chiefest charm for me,
And I prefer to cheat—you hear me shout!

HAPPY HUNTY:

My chief, you do but echo back my thoughts:
This competition is the death of trade.
'Tis plain (unless we wish to go to work)
Some other business we must early find.
What shall it be? The field of usefulness
Is yearly narrowing with the advance
Of wealth and population on this coast.
There's little left that any man can do
Without some other fellow stepping in
And doing it as well. If one essay
To pick a pocket he is sure to feel
(With what disgust I need not say to you)
Another hand inserted in the same.
You crack a crib at dead of night, and lo!
As you explore the dining-room for plate
You find in session there a graceless band
Stuffing their coats with spoons, their skins with wine.
And so it goes. Why, even undertake

To salt a mine and you will find it rich
With noble specimens placed there before!

LELAND THE KID:

And yet this line of immigration has
Advantages superior to aught
That elsewhere offers: all these passengers,
If punched with care—

COWBOY CHARLEY:

                  Significant remark!
It opens up a prospect wide and fair,
Suggesting to the thoughtful mind—*my* mind—
A scheme that is the boss lay-out. Instead
Of stopping passengers, let's carry them.
Instead of crying out: "Throw up your hands!"
Let's say: "Walk up and buy a ticket!" Why
Should we unwieldly goods and bullion take,
Watches and all such trifles, when we might
Far better charge their value three times o'er
For carrying them to market?

LELAND THE KID:

                      Put it there,
Old son!

HAPPY HUNTY:

          You take the cake, my dear. We'll build
A mighty railroad through this pass, and then
The stage folk will come up to us and squeal,
And say: "It is bad medicine for both;
What will you give or take?" And then we'll sell.

COWBOY CHARLEY:

Enlarge your notions, little one; this is
No petty, slouching, opposition scheme,
To be bought off like honest men and fools;
Mine eye prophetic pierces through the mists

That cloud the future, and I seem to see
A well-devised and executed scheme
Of wholesale robbery within the law
(Made by ourselves)—great, permanent, sublime,
And strong to grapple with the public throat—
Shaking the stuffing from the public purse,
The tears from bankrupt merchants' eyes, the blood
From widows' famished carcasses, the bread
From orphans' mouths!

HAPPY HUNTY:

Hooray!

LELAND THE KID:

Hooray!

ALL:

Hooray!

(They tear the masks from their faces, and discharging their shot-guns, throw them into the chaparral. Then they join hands, dance and sing the following song):

Ah! blessed to measure
The glittering treasure!
Ah! blessed to heap up the gold
Untold
That flows in a wide
And deepening tide—
Rolled, rolled, rolled
From multifold sources,
Converging its courses
Upon our—

LELAND THE KID:

Just wait a bit, my pards: I seem to hear
A sneaking grizzly cracking the dry twigs.
Such an intrusion might deprive the State
Of all the good that we intend it. Ha!

(Enter Sootymug. He saunters carelessly in and gracefully leans his back against a redwood.)

SOOTYMUG:

My boys, I thought I heard
　　Some careless revelry,
As if your minds were stirred
　　By some new devilry.
I too am in that line. Indeed, the mission
On which I come—

HAPPY HUNTY:

　　Here's more damned competition!

(Curtain)

Selections from

FANTASTIC FABLES

THE CRIMSON CANDLE

A Man lying at the point of death called his wife to his bedside and said:

"I am about to leave you forever; give me, therefore, one last proof of your affection and fidelity. In my desk you will find a crimson candle, which has been blessed by the High Priest and has a peculiar mystical significance. Swear to me that while it is in existence you will not remarry."

The Woman swore and the Man died. At the funeral the Woman stood at the head of the bier, holding a lighted crimson candle till it was wasted entirely away.

THE CONSCIENTIOUS OFFICIAL *reversed*

While a Division Superintendent of a railway was attending closely to his business of placing obstructions on the track and tampering with the switches he received word that the President of the road was about to discharge him for incompetency.

"Good Heavens!" he cried; "there are more accidents on my division than on all the rest of the line."

"The President is very particular," said the Man who brought him the news; "he thinks the same loss of life might be effected with less damage to the company's property."

"Does he expect me to shoot passengers through the car windows?" exclaimed the indignant official, spiking a loose tie across the rails. "Does he take me for an assassin?"

TREASURY AND ARMS

A Public Treasury, feeling Two Arms lifting out its contents, exclaimed:

"Mr. Shareman, I move for a division."

"You seem to know something about parliamentary forms of speech," said the Two Arms.

"Yes," replied the Public Treasury, "I am familiar with the hauls of legislation."

THE CRITICS

While bathing, Antinoüs was seen by Minerva, who was so enamoured of his beauty that, all armed as she happened to be, she descended from Olympus to woo him; but unluckily displaying her shield with the head of Medusa on it, she had the unhappiness to see the beautiful mortal turn to stone from catching a glimpse of it. She straightway ascended to ask Jove to restore him; but before this could be done a Sculptor and a Critic passed that way and espied him.

"This is a very bad Apollo," said the Sculptor: "the chest is too narrow, and one arm is at least a half-inch shorter than the other. The attitude is unnatural, and I may say impossible. Ah! my friend, you should see my statue of Antinoüs."

"In my judgment," said the Critic, "the figure is tolerably good, though rather Etrurian, but the expression of the face is decidedly Tuscan, and therefore false to nature. By the way, have you read my work on 'The Fallaciousness of the Aspectual in Art'?"

A CALL TO QUIT

Seeing that his audiences were becoming smaller every Sunday, a Minister of the Gospel broke off in the midst of a sermon, descended the pulpit stairs and walked on his hands down the central aisle of the church. He then re-mounted his feet, ascended to the pulpit and resumed his discourse, making no allusion to the incident.

"Now," said he to himself as he went home, "I shall have, henceforth, a large attendance and no snoring."

But on the following Friday he was waited upon by the Pillars of the Church, who informed him that in order to be in harmony with the New Theology and get full advantage of modern methods of Gospel interpretation they had deemed it advisable to make a change. They had therefore sent a call to Brother Jowjeetum-Fallal, the world-renowned Hindoo human pin-wheel, then holding forth in Hoopitup's circus. They were happy to say that the reverend gentleman had been moved by the Spirit to accept the call, and on the ensuing Sabbath would break the bread of life for the brethren or break his neck in the attempt.

THE DISCONTENTED MALEFACTOR

A Judge having sentenced a Malefactor to the penitentiary was proceeding to point out to him the disadvantages of crime and the profit of reformation.

"Your Honor," said the Malefactor, interrupting, "would you be kind enough to alter my punishment to ten years in the penitentiary and nothing else?"

"Why," said the Judge, surprised, "I have given you only three years!"

"Yes, I know," assented the Malefactor—"three years' imprisonment and the preaching. If you please, I should like to commute the preaching."

FATHER AND SON

"My boy," said an aged Father to his fiery and disobedient Son, "a hot temper is the soil of remorse. Promise me that when next you are angry you will count one hundred before you move or speak."

No sooner had the Son promised than he received a stinging blow from the paternal walking-stick, and by the time he had counted to seventy-five had the unhappiness to see the old man jump into a waiting cab and whirl away.

THE FOOLISH WOMAN

A Married Woman, whose lover was about to reform by running away, procured a pistol and shot him dead.

"Why did you do that, madam?" inquired a Policeman, sauntering by.

"Because," replied the Married Woman, "he was a wicked man, and had purchased a ticket to Chicago."

"My sister," said an adjacent Man of God, solemnly, "you cannot stop the wicked from going to Chicago by killing them."

MAN AND LIGHTNING

A Man Running for Office was overtaken by Lightning.

"You see," said the Lightning, as it crept past him inch by inch, "I can travel considerably faster than you."

"Yes," the Man Running for Office replied, "but think how much longer I keep going!"

THE LASSOED BEAR

A Hunter who had lassoed a Bear was trying to disengage himself from the rope, but the slip-knot about his wrist would not yield, for the Bear was all the time pulling in the slack with his paws. In the midst of his trouble the Hunter saw a Showman passing by and managed to attract his attention.

"What will you give me," he said, "for my Bear?"

"It will be some five or ten minutes," said the Showman, "before I shall want a bear, and it looks to me as if prices would fall during that time. I think I'll wait and watch the market."

"The price of this animal," the Hunter replied, "is down to bed-rock; you can have him for a cent a pound, spot cash, and I'll throw in the next one that I lasso. But the purchaser must remove the goods from the premises forthwith, to make room for three man-eating tigers, a cat-headed gorilla and an armful of rattlesnakes."

But the Showman passed on in maiden meditation, fancy free, and being joined soon afterward by the Bear, who was absently picking his teeth, it was inferred that they were not unacquainted.

THE WOODEN GUNS

An Artillery Regiment of a State Militia applied to the Governor for wooden guns to practice with.

"Those," they explained, "will be cheaper than real ones."

"It shall not be said that I sacrificed efficiency to economy," said the Governor. "You shall have real guns."

"Thank you, thank you," cried the warriors, effusively. "We will take good care of them, and in the event of war return them to the arsenal."

THE HOLY DEACON

An Itinerant Preacher who had wrought hard in the moral vineyard for several hours whispered to a Holy Deacon of the local church:

"Brother, these people know you, and your active support will bear fruit abundantly. Please pass the plate for me, and you shall have one fourth."

The Holy Deacon did so, and putting the money into his pocket waited till the congregation was dismissed, then said good-night.

"But the money, brother, the money that you collected!" said the Itinerant Preacher.

"Nothing is coming to you," was the reply; "the Adversary has hardened their hearts and one fourth is all they gave."

A HASTY SETTLEMENT

"Your Honor," said an Attorney, rising, "what is the present status of this case—as far as it has gone?"

"I have given a judgment for the residuary legatee under the will," said the Court, "put the costs upon the contestants, decided all questions relating to fees and other charges; and, in short, the estate in litigation has been settled, with all controversies, disputes, misunderstandings and differences of opinion thereunto appertaining."

"Ah, yes, I see," said the Attorney, thoughtfully, "we are making progress—we are getting on famously."

"Progress?" echoed the Judge—"progress? Why, sir, the matter is concluded!"

"Exactly, exactly; it had to be concluded in order to give relevancy to the motion that I am about to make. Your Honor, I move that the judgment of the Court be set aside and the case reopened."

"Upon what ground, sir?" the Judge asked in surprise.

"Upon the ground," said the Attorney, "that after paying all fees and expenses of litigation and all charges against the estate there will still be something left."

"There may have been an error," said his Honor, thoughtfully—"the Court may have underestimated the value of the estate. The motion is taken under advisement."

THE MAN WITH NO ENEMIES

An Inoffensive Person walking in a public place was assaulted by a Stranger with a Club, and severely beaten.

When the Stranger with a Club was brought to trial, the complainant said to the Judge:

"I do not know why I was assaulted; I have not an enemy in the world."

"That," said the defendant, "is why I struck him."

"Let the prisoner be discharged," said the Judge; "a man who has no enemies has no friends. The courts are not for such."

THE FLYING-MACHINE

An Ingenious Man who had built a flying-machine invited a great concourse of people to see it go up. At the appointed moment, everything being ready, he boarded the car and turned on the power. The machine immediately broke through the massive substructure upon which it was builded, and sank out of sight into the earth, the aeronaut springing out barely in time to save himself.

"Well," said he, "I have done enough to demonstrate the correctness of my details. The defects," he added, with a look at the ruined brick-work, "are merely basic and fundamental."

On this assurance the people came forward with subscriptions to build a second machine.

THE PARTY OVER THERE

A Man in a Hurry, whose watch was at his lawyer's, asked a Grave Person the time of day.

"I heard you ask that Party Over There the same question," said the Grave Person. "What answer did he give you?"

"He said it was about three o'clock," replied the Man in a Hurry; "but he did not look at his watch, and as the sun is nearly down I think it is later."

"The fact that the sun is nearly down," the Grave Person said, "is immaterial, but the fact that he did not consult his timepiece and make answer after due deliberation and consideration is fatal. The answer given," continued the Grave Person, consulting his own timepiece, "is of no effect, invalid, and void."

"What, then," said the Man in a Hurry, eagerly, "is the time of day?"

"The question is remanded to the Party Over There for a new answer," replied the Grave Person, returning his watch to his pocket and moving away with great dignity.

He was a Judge of an Appellate Court.

THE BUMBO OF JIAM

The Pahdour of Patagascar and the Gookul of Madagonia were disputing about an island that both claimed. Finally, at the suggestion of the International League of Cannon Founders, which had important branches in both countries, they decided to refer their claims to the Bumbo of Jiam, and abide by his judgment. In settling the preliminaries of the arbitration they had, however, the misfortune to disagree, and appealed to arms. At the end of a long and disastrous war, when both sides were exhausted and bankrupt, the Bumbo of Jiam intervened in the interest of peace.

"My great and good friends," he said to his brother sovereigns, "it will be advantageous to you to learn that some questions are more complex and perilous than others, presenting a greater number of points upon which it is possible to differ. For four generations your royal predecessors disputed about possession of that island without falling out. Beware, oh, beware the perils of international arbitration!—

against which I feel it my duty to protect you henceforth."

So saying, he annexed both countries, and after a long, peaceful and happy reign was poisoned by his Prime Minister.

LEGISLATOR AND SOAP

A member of the Kansas Legislature meeting a Cake of Soap was passing it by without recognition, but the Cake of Soap insisted on stopping and shaking hands. Thinking it might possibly be in the enjoyment of the elective franchise, he gave it a cordial and earnest grasp. On letting it go he observed that a part of it adhered to his fingers, and running to a brook in great alarm, proceeded to wash it off. In doing so he necessarily got some on the other hand, and when he had finished washing both were so white that he went to bed and sent for a physician.

THE HONEST CADI

A Robber who had plundered a merchant of one thousand pieces of gold was taken before the Cadi, who asked him if he had anything to say why he should not be decapitated.

"Your Honor," said the Robber, "I could do no otherwise than take the money, for Allah made me that way."

"Your defence is ingenious and sound," said the Cadi, "and I must acquit you of criminality. Unfortunately, Allah has also made me so that I must take off your head—unless," he added, thoughtfully, "you offer me a half of the gold; for He made me weak under temptation."

Thereupon the Robber put five hundred pieces of gold into the Cadi's hand.

"Good," said the Cadi. "I shall now remove only one-half your head. To show my trust in your discretion I shall leave intact the half that you talk with."

KANGAROO AND ZEBRA

A Kangaroo hopping awkwardly along with some bulky object concealed in her pouch met a Zebra, and desirous of keeping his attention upon himself, said:

"Your costume looks as if you might have come out of the penitentiary."

"Appearances are deceitful," replied the Zebra, smiling in the consciousness of a more insupportable wit, "or I should have to think that you had come out of the Legislature."

THE RETURNED CALIFORNIAN

A Man was hanged by the neck until he was dead. This was in 1893.

"Whence do you come?" Saint Peter asked when the Man presented himself at the gate of Heaven.

"From California," replied the applicant.

"Enter, my son, enter; you bring joyous tidings."

When the Man had vanished inside, Saint Peter took his memorandum tablet and made the following entry:

"February 16, 1893. California settled by the Christians."

THE DEVOTED WIDOW

A Widow weeping on her husband's grave was approached by an Engaging Gentleman who, in a respectful manner, assured her that he had long entertained for her the most tender feelings.

"Wretch!" cried the Widow. "Leave me this instant! Is this a time to talk to me of love?"

"I assure you, madam, that I had not intended to disclose my affection," the Engaging Gentleman humbly explained, "but the power of your beauty has overcome my discretion."

"You should see me when I have not been weeping," said the Widow.

DOG AND DOCTOR

A Dog that had seen a Doctor attending the burial of a wealthy patient, said: "When do you expect to dig it up?"

"Why should I dig it up?" the Doctor asked.

"When I bury a bone," said the Dog, "it is with an intention to uncover it later and pick it."

"The bones that I bury," said the Doctor, "are those that I can no longer pick."

AT HEAVEN'S GATE

Having risen from the tomb, a Woman presented herself at the gate of Heaven, and knocked with a trembling hand.

"Madam," said Saint Peter, rising and approaching the wicket, "whence do you come?"

"From San Francisco," replied the Woman, with embarrassment, as great beads of perspiration spangled her spiritual brow.

"Never mind, my good girl," the Saint said, compassionately. "Eternity is a long time; you can live that down."

"But that, if you please, is not all." The Woman was growing more and more confused. "I poisoned my husband. I chopped up my babies. I——"

"Ah," said the Saint, with sudden austerity, "your confession suggests a grave possibility. Were you a member of the Women's Press Association?"

The lady drew herself up and replied with warmth:

"I was not."

The gates of pearl and jasper swung back upon their golden hinges, making the most ravishing music, and the Saint, stepping aside, bowed low, saying:

"Enter, then, into thine eternal rest."

But the Woman hesitated.

"The poisoning—the chopping—the—the—" she stammered.

"Of no consequence, I assure you. We are not going to be

hard on a lady who did not belong to the Women's Press Association. Take a harp."

"But I applied for membership—I was blackballed."

"Take two harps."

SAINT AND SINNER

"My friend," said a distinguished officer of the Salvation Army to a Most Wicked Sinner, "I was once a drunkard, a thief, an assassin. The Divine Grace has made me what I am."

The Most Wicked Sinner looked at him from head to foot. "Henceforth," he said, "the Divine Grace, I fancy, will let well enough alone."

HIGHWAYMAN AND TRAVELER

A Highwayman confronted a Traveler, and covering him with a firearm, shouted: "Your money or your life!"

"My good friend," said the Traveler, "according to the terms of your demand my money will save my life, my life my money; you imply that you will take one or the other, but not both. If that is what you mean please be good enough to take my life."

"That is not what I mean," said the Highwayman; "you cannot save your money by giving up your life."

"Then take it anyhow," the Traveler said. "If it will not save my money it is good for nothing."

The Highwayman was so pleased with the Traveler's philosophy and wit that he took him into partnership and this splendid combination of talent started a newspaper.

A NEEDLESS LABOR

After waiting many a weary day to revenge himself upon a Lion for some unconsidered manifestation of contempt, a Skunk finally saw him coming and posting himself in the path ahead uttered the inaudible discord of his race. Observing that the Lion gave no attention to the matter, the Skunk, keeping carefully out of reach, said:

"Sir, I beg leave to point out that I have set on foot an implacable odor."

"My dear fellow," the Lion replied, "you have taken a needless trouble; I already knew that you are not a rose."

A DEFECTIVE PETITION

An Associate Justice of the Supreme Court was sitting by a river when a Traveler approached and said:

"I wish to cross. Will it be lawful to use this boat?"

"It will," was the reply; "it is my boat."

The Traveler thanked him, and pushing the boat into the water embarked and rowed away. But the boat sank and he was drowned.

"Heartless man!" said an Indignant Spectator. "Why did you not tell him that your boat had a hole in it?"

"The matter of the boat's condition," said the great jurist, "was not brought before me."

TWO SONS

A Man had Two Sons. The elder was virtuous and dutiful, the younger wicked and crafty. When the father was about to die, he called them before him and said: "I have only two things of value—my herd of camels and my blessing. How shall I allot them?"

"Give to me," said the Younger Son, "thy blessing, for it may reform me. The camels I should be sure to sell and squander the money."

The Elder Son, disguising his joy, said that he would try to be content with the camels and a pious mind.

It was so arranged and the Man died. Then the wicked Younger Son went before the Cadi and said: "Behold, my brother has defrauded me of my lawful heritage. He is so bad that our father, as is well known, denied him his blessing; is it likely that he gave him the camels?"

So the Elder Son was compelled to give up the herd and was soundly bastinadoed for his rapacity.

DIPLOMACY

"If you do not submit my claim to arbitration," wrote the President of Omohu to the President of Modugy, "I shall take immediate steps to collect it in my own way!"

"Sir," replied the President of Modugy, "you may go to the devil with your threat of war."

"My great and good friend," wrote the other, "you mistake the character of my communication. It is an antepenultimatum."

A FAULTY PERFORMANCE

A pet Opossum belonging to a Great Critic stole his favorite kitten and was about to kill and eat it when she saw him approaching, and fearing detection she concealed it in her pouch.

"Well, my pretty one," said the Great Critic, with condescension, "what new charms and graces have you to-day?"

Before she could reply the kitten set up a diligent and persistent mewing. When at last the music had ceased the Opossum said:

"I've been dabbling a little in mimicry and ventriloquism; I thought it would please you, sir."

"The desire to please is ever pleasing," the Great Critic answered, not without a touch of professional dignity, "but you have much to learn about the mewing of kittens."

THE MAIN THING

A Poet proffering his work to an Editor said:

"This is a small poem, but quality is the main thing. I venture to think you'll find it true poetry."

Having read it the Editor put it into a drawer and handing the Poet a ten-cent piece said:

"This is a smallish coin, but I am so bold as to hope that you will be pleased with its purity. It is nearly all silver."

THE INCONSOLABLE WIDOW

A Woman in widow's weeds was weeping upon a grave.

"Console yourself, madam," said a Sympathetic Stranger. "Heaven's mercies are infinite. There is another man somewhere, besides your husband, with whom you can still be happy."

"There was," she sobbed—"there was, but this is his grave."

Selections from

AESOPUS EMENDATUS

FOX AND GRAPES

A Fox, seeing some sour grapes hanging within an inch of his nose, and being unwilling to admit that there was anything he would not eat, solemnly declared that they were out of his reach.

WOLVES AND DOGS

"Why should there be strife between us?" said the Wolves to the Sheep. "It is all owing to those meddlesome dogs. Dismiss them, and we shall have peace."

"You seem," replied the Sheep, "to think it an easy thing to dismiss dogs."

DAME FORTUNE AND THE TRAVELER

A weary Traveler who had lain down and fallen asleep on the brink of a deep well was discovered by Dame Fortune.

"If this fool," she said, "should have an uneasy dream and

roll into the well men would say that I did it. It is painful to me to be unjustly accused, and I shall see that I am not." So saying she rolled the man into the well.

MAN AND GOOSE

"See these valuable golden eggs," said a Man that owned a Goose. "Surely a Goose that can lay such eggs must have a gold mine inside her."

So he killed the Goose and cut her open, but found that she was just like any other goose. Moreover, on examining the eggs that she had laid he found they were just like any other eggs.

self deceived but went too far spread the truth

JUPITER AND THE BIRDS

Jupiter commanded all the birds to appear before him, so that he might choose the most beautiful to be their king. The ugly Jackdaw, collecting all the fine feathers that had fallen from the other birds, attached them to his own body and appeared at the examination, looking very gay. The other birds recognizing their own borrowed plumage indignantly protested and began to strip him.

"Hold!" said Jupiter; "this self-made bird has more sense than any of you. He shall be your king."

Selections from

NEGLIGIBLE TALES

A BOTTOMLESS GRAVE

My name is John Brenwalter. My father, a drunkard, had a patent for an invention for making coffee-berries out of clay; but he was an honest man and would not himself engage in the manufacture. He was, therefore, only moderately wealthy, his royalties from his really valuable invention bringing him hardly enough to pay his expenses of litigation with rogues guilty of infringement. So I lacked many advantages enjoyed by the children of unscrupulous and dishonorable parents, and had it not been for a noble and devoted mother, who neglected all my brothers and sisters and personally supervised my education, should have grown up in ignorance and been compelled to teach school. To be the favorite child of a good woman is better than gold.

When I was nineteen years of age my father had the misfortune to die. He had always had perfect health, and his death, which occurred at the dinner table without a moment's warning, surprised no one more than himself. He had that very morning been notified that a patent had been granted him for a device to burst open safes by hydraulic pressure, without noise. The Commissioner of Patents had pronounced it the most ingenious, effective and generally meritorious invention that had ever been submitted to him, and my father had naturally looked forward to an old age of prosperity and honor. His sudden death was, therefore, a deep disappointment to him; but my mother, whose piety and resignation to the will of Heaven were conspicuous virtues of her character, was apparently less affected. At the close of the meal, when my poor father's body had been removed from the floor, she called us all into an adjoining room and addressed us as follows:

"My children, the uncommon occurrence that you have just witnessed is one of the most disagreeable incidents in a good man's life, and one in which I take little pleasure, I assure you. I beg you to believe that I had no hand in bringing it about. Of course," she added, after a pause, during which her eyes were cast down in deep thought, "of course it is better that he is dead."

She uttered this with so evident a sense of its obviousness as a self-evident truth that none of us had the courage to brave her surprise by asking an explanation. My mother's air of surprise when any of us went wrong in any way was very terrible to us. One day, when in a fit of peevish temper, I had taken the liberty to cut off the baby's ear, her simple words, "John, you surprise me!" appeared to me so sharp a reproof that after a sleepless night I went to her in tears, and throwing myself at her feet, exclaimed: "Mother, forgive me for surprising you." So now we all—including the one-eared baby—felt that it would keep matters smoother to accept without question the statement that it was better, somehow, for our dear father to be dead. My mother continued:

"I must tell you, my children, that in a case of sudden and mysterious death the law requires the Coroner to come and cut the body into pieces and submit them to a number of men who, having inspected them, pronounce the person dead. For this the Coroner gets a large sum of money. I wish to avoid that painful formality in this instance; it is one which never had the approval of—of the remains. John" —here my mother turned her angel face to me—"you are an educated lad, and very discreet. You have now an opportunity to show your gratitude for all the sacrifices that your education has entailed upon the rest of us. John, go and remove the Coroner."

Inexpressibly delighted by this proof of my mother's

confidence, and by the chance to distinguish myself by an act that squared with my natural disposition, I knelt before her, carried her hand to my lips and bathed it with tears of sensibility. Before five o'clock that afternoon I had removed the Coroner.

I was immediately arrested and thrown into jail, where I passed a most uncomfortable night, being unable to sleep because of the profanity of my fellow-prisoners, two clergymen, whose theological training had given them a fertility of impious ideas and a command of blasphemous language altogether unparalleled. But along toward morning the jailer, who, sleeping in an adjoining room, had been equally disturbed, entered the cell and with a fearful oath warned the reverend gentlemen that if he heard any more swearing their sacred calling would not prevent him from turning them into the street. After that they moderated their objectionable conversation, substituting an accordion, and I slept the peaceful and refreshing sleep of youth and innocence.

The next morning I was taken before the Superior Judge, sitting as a committing magistrate, and put upon my preliminary examination. I pleaded not guilty, adding that the man whom I had murdered was a notorious Democrat. (My good mother was a Republican, and from early childhood I had been carefully instructed by her in the principles of honest government and the necessity of suppressing factional opposition.) The Judge, elected by a Republican ballot-box with a sliding bottom, was visibly impressed by the cogency of my plea and offered me a cigarette.

"May it please your Honor," began the District Attorney, "I do not deem it necessary to submit any evidence in this case. Under the law of the land you sit here as a committing magistrate. It is therefore your duty to commit. Testimony and argument alike would imply a doubt that your Honor means to perform your sworn duty. That is my case."

My counsel, a brother of the deceased Coroner, rose and said: "May it please the Court, my learned friend on the other side has so well and eloquently stated the law governing in this case that it only remains for me to inquire to what extent it has been already complied with. It is

true, your Honor is a committing magistrate, and as such
it is your duty to commit—what? That is a matter which the
law has wisely and justly left to your own discretion, and
wisely you have discharged already every obligation that
the law imposes. Since I have known your Honor you have
done nothing but commit. You have committed embracery,
theft, arson, perjury, adultery, murder—every crime in the
calendar and every excess known to the sensual and de-
praved, including my learned friend, the District Attorney.
You have done your whole duty as a committing magistrate,
and as there is no evidence against this worthy young man,
my client, I move that he be discharged."

An impressive silence ensued. The Judge arose, put on the
black cap and in a voice trembling with emotion sentenced
me to life and liberty. Then turning to my counsel he said,
coldly but significantly:

"I will see you later."

The next morning the lawyer who had so conscientiously
defended me against a charge of murdering his own
brother—with whom he had a quarrel about some land—had
disappeared and his fate is to this day unknown.

In the meantime my poor father's body had been secretly
buried at midnight in the back yard of his late residence,
with his late boots on and the contents of his late stomach
unanalyzed. "He was opposed to display," said my dear
mother, as she finished tamping down the earth above him
and assisted the children to litter the place with straw;
"his instincts were all domestic and he loved a quiet life."

My mother's application for letters of administration
stated that she had good reason to believe that the deceased
was dead, for he had not come home to his meals for several
days; but the Judge of the Crowbait Court—as she ever
afterward contemptuously called it—decided that the proof
of death was insufficient, and put the estate into the hands
of the Public Administrator, who was his son-in-law. It was
found that the liabilities were exactly balanced by the as-
sets; there was left only the patent for the device for burst-
ing open safes without noise, by hydraulic pressure and this
had passed into the ownership of the Probate Judge and the
Public Administraitor—as my dear mother preferred to spell

it. Thus, within a few brief months a worthy and respectable family was reduced from prosperity to crime; necessity compelled us to go to work.

In the selection of occupations we were governed by a variety of considerations, such as personal fitness, inclination, and so forth. My mother opened a select private school for instruction in the art of changing the spots upon leopard-skin rugs; my eldest brother, George Henry, who had a turn for music, became a bugler in a neighboring asylum for deaf mutes; my sister, Mary Maria, took orders for Professor Pumpernickel's Essence of Latchkeys for flavoring mineral springs, and I set up as an adjuster and gilder of crossbeams for gibbets. The other children, too young for labor, continued to steal small articles exposed in front of shops, as they had been taught.

In our intervals of leisure we decoyed travelers into our house and buried the bodies in a cellar.

In one part of this cellar we kept wines, liquors and provisions. From the rapidity of their disappearance we acquired the superstitious belief that the spirits of the persons buried there came at dead of night and held a festival. It was at least certain that frequently of a morning we would discover fragments of pickled meats, canned goods and such débris, littering the place, although it had been securely locked and barred against human intrusion. It was proposed to remove the provisions and store them elsewhere, but our dear mother, always generous and hospitable, said it was better to endure the loss than risk exposure: if the ghosts were denied this trifling gratification they might set on foot an investigation, which would overthrow our scheme of the division of labor, by diverting the energies of the whole family into the single industry pursued by me—we might all decorate the cross-beams of gibbets. We accepted her decision with filial submission, due to our reverence for her worldly wisdom and the purity of her character.

One night while we were all in the cellar—none dared to enter it alone—engaged in bestowing upon the Mayor of an adjoining town the solemn offices of Christian burial, my mother and the younger children, holding a candle each, while George Henry and I labored with a spade and pick, my sister Mary Maria uttered a shriek and covered her eyes with her hands. We were all dreadfully startled and the Mayor's obsequies were instantly suspended, while with pale faces and in trembling tones we begged her to say what had alarmed her. The younger children were so agitated that they held their candles unsteadily, and the waving shadows of our figures danced with uncouth and grotesque movements on the walls and flung themselves into the most uncanny attitudes. The face of the dead man, now gleaming ghastly in the light, and now extinguished by some floating shadow, appeared at each emergence to have taken on a new and more forbidding expression, a maligner menace. Frightened even more than ourselves by the girl's scream, rats raced in multitudes about the place, squeaking shrilly, or starred the black opacity of some distant corner with steadfast eyes, mere points of green light, matching the faint phosphorescence of decay that filled the half-dug grave and seemed the visible manifestation of that faint odor of mortality which tainted the unwholesome air. The children now sobbed and clung about the limbs of their elders, dropping their candles, and we were near being left in total darkness, except for that sinister light, which slowly welled upward from the disturbed earth and overflowed the edges of the grave like a fountain.

Meanwhile my sister, crouching in the earth that had been thrown out of the excavation, had removed her hands from her face and was staring with expanded eyes into an obscure space between two wine casks.

"There it is!—there it is!" she shrieked, pointing; "God in heaven! can't you see it?"

And there indeed it was!—a human figure, dimly discernible in the gloom—a figure that wavered from side to side as if about to fall, clutching at the wine-casks for support, had stepped unsteadily forward and for one moment stood revealed in the light of our remaining candles; then it surged heavily and fell prone upon the earth. In that moment we had all recognized the figure, the face and bearing of our father—dead these ten months and buried by our own hands!—our father indubitably risen and ghastly drunk!

On the incidents of our precipitate flight from that horrible place—on the extinction of all human sentiment in that tumultuous, mad scramble up the damp and mouldy stairs—slipping, falling, pulling one another down and clambering over one another's back—the lights extinguished, babes trampled beneath the feet of their strong brothers and hurled backward to death by a mother's arm!—on all this I do not dare to dwell. My mother, my eldest brother and sister and I escaped; the others remained below, to perish of their wounds, or of their terror—some, perhaps, by flame. For within an hour we four, hastily gathering together what money and jewels we had and what clothing we could carry, fired the dwelling and fled by its light into the hills. We did not even pause to collect the insurance, and my dear mother said on her death-bed, years afterward in a distant land, that this was the only sin of omission that lay upon her conscience. Her confessor, a holy man, assured her that under the circumstances Heaven would pardon the neglect.

About ten years after our removal from the scenes of my childhood I, then a prosperous forger, returned in disguise to the spot with a view to obtaining, if possible, some treasure belonging to us, which had been buried in the cellar. I may say that I was unsuccessful: the discovery of many human bones in the runs had set the authorities digging for more. They had found the treasure and had kept it for their honesty. The house had not been rebuilt; the whole suburb was, in fact, a desolation. So many unearthly sights and sounds had been reported thereabout that nobody would live there. As there was none to question nor molest, I resolved to gratify my filial piety by gazing once more upon the face of my beloved father, if indeed our eyes had deceived us and he was still in his grave. I remembered, too, that he had always worn an enormous diamond ring, and never having seen it nor heard of it since his death, I had reason to think he might have been buried in it. Procuring a spade, I soon located the grave in what had been the backyard and began digging. When I had got down about four feet the whole bottom fell out of the grave and I was precipitated into a large drain, falling through a long hole in its crumbling arch. There was no body, nor any vestige of one.

Unable to get out of the excavation, I crept through the drain, and having with some difficulty removed a mass of charred rubbish and blackened masonry that choked it, emerged into what had been that fateful cellar.

All was clear. My father, whatever had caused him to be "taken bad" at his meal (and I think my sainted mother could have thrown some light upon that matter) had indubitably been buried alive. The grave having been accidentally dug above the forgotten drain, and down almost to the crown of its arch, and no coffin having been used, his struggles on reviving had broken the rotten masonry and he had fallen through, escaping finally into the cellar. Feeling that he was not welcome in his own house, yet having no other, he had lived in subterranean seclusion, a witness to our thrift and a pensioner on our providence. It was he who had eaten our food; it was he who had drunk our wine—he was no better than a thief! In a moment of intoxication, and feeling, no doubt, that need of companionship which is the one sympathetic link between a drunken man and his race, he had left his place of concealment at a strangely inopportune time, entailing the most deplorable consequences upon those nearest and dearest to him—a blunder that had almost the dignity of crime.

THE WIDOWER TURMORE

The circumstances under which Joram Turmore became a widower have never been popularly understood. I know them, naturally, for I am Joram Turmore; and my wife, the late Elizabeth Mary Turmore, is by no means ignorant of them; but although she doubtless relates them, yet they remain a secret, for not a soul has ever believed her.

When I married Elizabeth Mary Johnin she was very wealthy, otherwise I could hardly have afforded to marry, for I had not a cent, and Heaven had not put into my heart any intention to earn one. I held the Professorship of Cats in the University of Graymaulkin, and scholastic pursuits had unfitted me for the heat and burden of business or

labor. Moreover, I could not forget that I was a Turmore—
a member of a family whose motto from the time of William
of Normandy has been *Laborare est errare*. The only known
infraction of the sacred family tradition occurred when Sir
Aldebaran Turmore de Peters-Turmore, an illustrious master
burglar of the seventeenth century, personally assisted at a
difficult operation undertaken by some of his workmen. That
blot upon our escutcheon cannot be contemplated without
the most poignant mortification.

My incumbency of the Chair of Cats in the Graymaulkin
University had not, of course, been marked by any instance
of mean industry. There had never, at any one time, been
more than two students of the Noble Science, and by merely
repeating the manuscript lectures of my predecessor, which
I had found among his effects (he died at sea on his way to
Malta) I could sufficiently sate their famine for knowledge
without really earning even the distinction which served
in place of salary.

Naturally, under the straitened circumstances, I regarded
Elizabeth Mary as a kind of special Providence. She unwisely refused to share her fortune with me, but for that I
cared nothing; for, although by the laws of that country (as
is well known) a wife has control of her separate property
during her life, it passes to the husband at her death; nor
can she dispose of it otherwise by will. The mortality among
wives is considerable, but not excessive.

Having married Elizabeth Mary and, as it were, ennobled
her by making her a Turmore, I felt that the manner of her
death ought, in some sense, to match her social distinction.
If I should remove her by any of the ordinary marital
methods I should incur a just reproach, as one destitute of
a proper family pride. Yet I could not hit upon a suitable
plan.

In this emergency I decided to consult the Turmore
archives, a priceless collection of documents, comprising the
records of the family from the time of its founder in the
seventh century of our era. I knew that among these sacred
muniments I should find detailed accounts of all the principal murders committed by my sainted ancestors for forty

generations. From that mass of papers I could hardly fail to derive the most valuable suggestions.

The collection contained also most interesting relics. There were patents of nobility granted to my forefathers for daring and ingenious removals of pretenders to thrones, or occupants of them; stars, crosses and other decorations attesting services of the most secret and unmentionable character; miscellaneous gifts from the world's greatest conspirators, representing an intrinsic money value beyond computation. There were robes, jewels, swords of honor, and every kind of "testimonials of esteem"; a king's skull fashioned into a wine cup; the title deeds to vast estates, long alienated by confiscation, sale, or abandonment; an illuminated breviary that had belonged to Sir Aldebaran Turmore de Peters-Turmore of accursed memory; embalmed ears of several of the family's most renowned enemies; the small intestine of a certain unworthy Italian statesman inimical to Turmores, which, twisted into a jumping rope, had served the youth of six kindred generations—mementoes and souvenirs precious beyond the appraisals of imagination, but by the sacred mandates of tradition and sentiment forever inalienable by sale or gift.

As the head of the family, I was custodian of all these priceless heirlooms, and for their safe keeping had constructed in the basement of my dwelling a strong-room of massive masonry, whose solid stone walls and single iron door could defy alike the earthquake's shock, the tireless assaults of Time, and Cupidity's unholy hand.

To this thesaurus of the soul, redolent of sentiment and tenderness, and rich in suggestions of crime, I now repaired for hints upon assassination. To my unspeakable astonishment and grief I found it empty! Every shelf, every chest, every coffer had been rifled. Of that unique and incomparable collection not a vestige remained! Yet I proved that until I had myself unlocked the massive metal door, not a bolt nor bar had been disturbed; the seals upon the lock had been intact.

I passed the night in alternate lamentation and research, equally fruitless; the mystery was impenetrable to conjecture, the pain invincible to balm. But never once through-

out that dreadful night did my firm spirit relinquish its high
design against Elizabeth Mary, and daybreak found me more
resolute than before to harvest the fruits of my marriage.
My great loss seemed but to bring me into nearer spiritual
relations with my dead ancestors, and to lay upon me a
new and more inevitable obedience to the suasion that spoke
in every globule of my blood.

My plan of action was soon formed, and procuring a
stout cord I entered my wife's bedroom, finding her, as I
expected, in a sound sleep. Before she was awake, I had her
bound fast, hand and foot. She was greatly surprised and
pained, but heedless of her remonstrances, delivered in a
high key, I carried her into the now rifled strong-room,
which I had never suffered her to enter, and of whose treasures I had not apprised her. Seating her, still bound, in an
angle of the wall, I passed the next two days and nights in
conveying bricks and mortar to the spot, and on the morning
of the third day had her securely walled in, from floor to
ceiling. All this time I gave no further heed to her pleas
for mercy than (on her assurance of non-resistance, which I
am bound to say she honorably observed) to grant her the
freedom of her limbs. The space allowed her was about four
feet by six. As I inserted the last bricks of the top course, in
contact with the ceiling of the strong-room, she bade me farewell with what I deemed the composure of despair, and I
rested from my work, feeling that I had faithfully observed
the traditions of an ancient and illustrious family. My only
bitter reflection, so far as my own conduct was concerned,
came of the consciousness that in the performance of my
design I had labored; but this no living soul would ever
know.

After a night's rest I went to the Judge of the Court of
Successions and Inheritances and made a true and sworn
relation of all that I had done—except that I ascribed to a
servant the manual labor of building the wall. His honor appointed a court commissioner, who made a careful examination of the work, and upon his report Elizabeth Mary
Turmore was, at the end of a week, formally pronounced
dead. By due process of law I was put into possession of her
estate, and although this was not by hundreds of thousands

of dollars as valuable as my lost treasures, it raised me from poverty to affluence and brought me the respect of the great and good.

Some six months after these events strange rumors reached me that the ghost of my deceased wife had been seen in several places about the country, but always at a considerable distance from Graymaulkin. These rumors, which I was unable to trace to any authentic source, differed widely in many particulars, but were alike in ascribing to the apparition a certain high degree of apparent worldly prosperity combined with an audacity most uncommon in ghosts. Not only was the spirit attired in most costly raiment, but it walked at noonday, and even drove! I was inexpressibly annoyed by these reports, and thinking there might be something more than superstition in the popular belief that only the spirits of the unburied dead still walk the earth, I took some workmen equipped with picks and crowbars into the now long unentered strong-room, and ordered them to demolish the brick wall that I had built about the partner of my joys. I was resolved to give the body of Elizabeth Mary such burial as I thought her immortal part might be willing to accept as an equivalent to the privilege of ranging at will among the haunts of the living.

In a few minutes we had broken down the wall and, thrusting a lamp through the breach, I looked in. Nothing! Not a bone, not a lock of hair, not a shred of clothing—the narrow space which, upon my affidavit, had been legally declared to hold all that was mortal of the late Mrs. Turmore was absolutely empty! This amazing disclosure, coming upon a mind already overwrought with too much of mystery and excitement, was more than I could bear. I shrieked aloud and fell in a fit. For months afterward I lay between life and death, fevered and delirious; nor did I recover until my physician had had the providence to take a case of valuable jewels from my safe and leave the country.

The next summer I had occasion to visit my wine cellar, in one corner of which I had built the now long disused strong-room. In moving a cask of Madeira I struck it with considerable force against the partition wall, and was surprised to observe that it displaced two large square stones forming a part of the wall.

Applying my hands to these, I easily pushed them out entirely, and looking through saw that they had fallen into the niche in which I had immured my lamented wife; facing the opening which their fall left, and at a distance of four feet, was the brickwork which my own hands had made for that unfortunate gentlewoman's restraint. At this significant revelation I began a search of the wine cellar. Behind a row of casks I found four historically interesting but intrinsically valueless objects:

First, the mildewed remains of a ducal robe of state (Florentine) of the eleventh century; second, an illuminated vellum breviary with the name of Sir Aldebaran Turmore de Peters-Turmore inscribed in colors on the title page; third, a human skull fashioned into a drinking cup and deeply stained with wine; fourth, the iron cross of a Knight Commander of the Imperial Austrian Order of Assassins by Poison.

That was all—not an object having commercial value, no papers—nothing. But this was enough to clear up the mystery of the strong-room. My wife had early divined the existence and purpose of that apartment, and with the skill amounting to genius had effected an entrance by loosening the two stones in the wall.

Through that opening she had at several times abstracted the entire collection, which doubtless she had succeeded in converting into coin of the realm. When with an unconscious justice which deprives me of all satisfaction in the memory I decided to build her into the wall, by some malign fatality I selected that part of it in which were these movable stones, and doubtless before I had fairly finished my bricklaying she had removed them and, slipping through into the wine cellar, replaced them as they were originally laid. From the cellar she had easily escaped unobserved, to enjoy her infamous gains in distant parts. I have endeavored to procure a warrant, but the Lord High Baron of the Court of Indictment and Conviction reminds me that she is legally dead, and says my only course is to go before the Master in Cadavery and move for a writ of disinterment and constructive revival. So it looks as if I must suffer without redress this great wrong at the hands of a woman devoid alike of principle and shame.

THE PARENTICIDE CLUB

MY FAVORITE MURDER

Having murdered my mother under circumstances of singular atrocity, I was arrested and put upon my trial, which lasted seven years. In charging the jury, the judge of the Court of Acquittal remarked that it was one of the most ghastly crimes that he had ever been called upon to explain away.

At this, my attorney rose and said:

"May it please your Honor, crimes are ghastly or agreeable only by comparison. If you were familiar with the details of my client's previous murder of his uncle you would discern in his later offense (if offense it may be called) something in the nature of tender forbearance and filial consideration for the feelings of the victim. The appalling ferocity of the former assassination was indeed inconsistent with any hypothesis but that of guilt; and had it not been for the fact that the honorable judge before whom he was tried was the president of a life insurance company that took risks on hanging, and in which my client held a policy, it is hard to see how he could decently have been acquitted. If your Honor would like to hear about it for instruction and guidance of your Honor's mind, this unfortunate man, my client, will consent to give himself the pain of relating it under oath."

The district attorney said: "Your Honor, I object. Such a statement would be in the nature of evidence, and the testimony in this case is closed. The prisoner's statement should have been introduced three years ago, in the spring of 1881."

"In a statutory sense," said the judge, "you are right, and in the Court of Objections and Technicalities you would get a ruling in your favor. But not in a Court of Acquittal. The objection is overruled."

"I except," said the district attorney.

"You cannot do that," the judge said. "I must remind you that in order to take an exception you must first get this case transferred for a time to the Court of Exceptions on a formal motion duly supported by affidavits. A motion to that effect by your predecessor in office was denied by me during the first year of this trial. Mr. Clerk, swear the prisoner."

The customary oath having been administered, I made the following statement, which impressed the judge with so strong a sense of the comparative triviality of the offense for which I was on trial that he made no further search for mitigating circumstances, but simply instructed the jury to acquit, and I left the court, without a stain on my reputation:

"I was born in 1856 in Kalamakee, Mich., of honest and reputable parents, one of whom Heaven has mercifully spared to comfort me in my later years. In 1867 the family came to California and settled near Nigger Head, where my father opened a road agency and prospered beyond the dreams of avarice. He was a reticent, saturnine man then, though his increasing years have now somewhat relaxed the austerity of his disposition, and I believe that nothing but his memory of the sad event for which I am now on trial prevents him from manifesting a genuine hilarity.

"Four years after we had set up the road agency an itinerant preacher came along, and having no other way to pay for the night's lodging that we gave him, favored us with an exhortation of such power that, praise God, we were all converted to religion. My father at once sent for his brother, the Hon. William Ridley of Stockton, and on his arrival turned over the agency to him, charging him nothing for the franchise nor plant—the latter consisting of a Winchester rifle, a sawed-off shotgun, and an assortment of masks made out of flour sacks. The family then moved to Ghost Rock and opened a dance house. It was called 'The Saints' Rest Hurdy-Gurdy,' and the proceedings each night began with prayer. It was there that my now sainted mother, by her grace in the dance, acquired the *sobriquet* of 'The Bucking Walrus.'

"In the fall of '75 I had occasion to visit Coyote, on the road to Mahala, and took the stage at Ghost Rock. There were four other passengers. About three miles beyond Nigger Head, persons whom I identified as my Uncle William and his two sons held up the stage. Finding nothing in the express box, they went through the passengers. I acted a most honorable part in the affair, placing myself in line with the others, holding up my hands and permitting myself to be deprived of forty dollars and a gold watch. From my behavior no one could have suspected that I knew the gentlemen who gave the entertainment. A few days later, when I went to Nigger Head and asked for the return of my money and watch my uncle and cousins swore they knew nothing of the matter, and they affected a belief that my father and I had done the job ourselves in dishonest violation of commercial good faith. Uncle William even threatened to retaliate by starting an opposition dance house at Ghost Rock. As 'The Saints' Rest' had become rather unpopular, I saw that this would assuredly ruin it and prove a paying enterprise, so I told my uncle that I was willing to overlook the past if he would take me into the scheme and keep the partnership a secret from my father. This fair offer he rejected, and I then perceived that it would be better and more satisfactory if he were dead.

"My plans to that end were soon perfected, and communicating them to my dear parents I had the gratification of receiving their approval. My father said he was proud of me, and my mother promised that although her religion forbade her to assist in taking human life I should have the advantage of her prayers for my success. As a preliminary measure looking to my security in case of detection I made an application for membership in that powerful order, the Knights of Murder, and in due course was received as a member of the Ghost Rock commandery. On the day that my probation ended I was for the first time permitted to inspect the records of the order and learn who belonged to it—all the rites of initiation having been conducted in masks. Fancy my delight when, in looking over the roll of membership, I found the third name to be that of my uncle, who indeed was junior vice-chancellor of the order! Here was an opportunity exceeding my wildest dreams—to murder I could add insubordination and treachery. It was what my good mother would have called 'a special Providence.'

"At about this time something occurred which caused my cup of joy, already full, to overflow on all sides, a circular cataract of bliss. Three men, strangers in that locality, were arrested for the stage robbery in which I had lost my money and watch. They were brought to trial and, despite my efforts to clear them and fasten the guilt upon three of the most respectable and worthy citizens of Ghost Rock, convicted on the clearest proof. The murder would now be as wanton and reasonless as I could wish.

"One morning I shouldered my Winchester rifle, and going over to my uncle's house, near Nigger Head, asked my Aunt Mary, his wife, if he were at home, adding that I had come to kill him. My aunt replied with her peculiar smile that so many gentlemen called on that errand and were afterward carried away without having performed it that I must excuse her for doubting my good faith in the matter. She said I did not look as if I would kill anybody, so, as a proof of good faith I leveled my rifle and wounded a Chinaman who happened to be passing the house. She said she knew whole families that could do a thing of that kind, but Bill Ridley was a horse of another color. She said, however, that I would find him over on the other side of the creek in the sheep lot; and she added that she hoped the best man would win.

"My Aunt Mary was one of the most fair-minded women that I have ever met.

"I found my uncle down on his knees engaged in skinning a sheep. Seeing that he had neither gun nor pistol handy I had not the heart to shoot him, so I approached him, greeted him pleasantly and struck him a powerful blow on the head with the butt of my rifle. I have a very good delivery and Uncle William lay down on his side, then rolled over on his back, spread out his fingers and shivered. Before he could recover the use of his limbs I seized the knife that he had been using and cut his hamstrings. You know, doubtless, that when you sever the *tendo Achillis* the patient has no further use of his leg; it is just the same as if he had no leg. Well, I parted them both, and when he revived he was at my service. As soon as he comprehended the situation, he said:

" 'Samuel, you have got the drop on me and can afford to be generous. I have only one thing to ask of you, and that is that you carry me to the house and finish me in the bosom of my family.'

"I told him I thought that a pretty reasonable request and I would do so if he would let me put him into a wheat sack; he would be easier to carry that way and if we were seen by the neighbors *en route* it would cause less remark. He agreed to that, and going to the barn I got a sack. This, however, did not fit him; it was too short and much wider than he; so I bent his legs, forced his knees up against his breast and got him into it that way, tying the sack above his head. He was a heavy man and I had all that I could do to get him on my back, but I staggered along for some distance until I came to a swing that some of the children had suspended to the branch of an oak. Here I laid him down and sat upon him to rest, and the sight of the rope gave me a happy inspiration. In twenty minutes my uncle, still in the sack, swung free to the sport of the wind.

"I had taken down the rope, tied one end tightly about the mouth of the bag, thrown the other across the limb and hauled him up about five feet from the ground. Fastening the other end of the rope also about the mouth of the sack, I had the satisfaction to see my uncle converted into a large, fine pendulum. I must add that he was not himself entirely aware of the nature of the change that he had undergone in his relation to the exterior world, though in justice to a good man's memory I ought to say that I do not think he would in any case have wasted much of my time in vain remonstrance.

"Uncle William had a ram that was famous in all that region as a fighter. It was in a state of chronic constitutional indignation. Some deep disappointment in early life had soured its disposition and it had declared war upon the whole world. To say that it would butt anything accessible is but faintly to express the nature and scope of its military activity: the universe was its antagonist; its methods that of a projectile. It fought like the angels and devils, in mid-air, cleaving the atmosphere like a bird, describing a parabolic curve and descending upon its victim at just the exact angle of incidence to make the most of its velocity and weight. Its momentum, calculated in foot-tons, was something incredible. It had been seen to destroy a four year old bull by a single impact upon that animal's gnarly forehead. No stone wall had ever been known to resist its downward swoop; there were no trees tough enough to stay it; it would splinter them into matchwood and defile their leafy honors in the dust. This irascible and implacable brute—this incarnate thunderbolt—this monster of the upper deep, I had seen reposing in the shade of an adjacent tree, dreaming dreams of conquest and glory. It was with a view to summoning it forth to the field of honor that I suspended its master in the manner described.

"Having completed my preparations, I imparted to the avuncular pendulum a gentle oscillation, and retiring to cover behind a contiguous rock, lifted up my voice in a long rasping cry whose diminishing final note was drowned in a noise like that of a swearing cat, which emanated from the sack. Instantly that formidable sheep was upon its feet and had taken in the military situation at a glance. In a few moments it had approached, stamping, to within fifty yards of the swinging foeman, who, now retreating and anon advancing, seemed to invite the fray. Suddenly I saw the beast's head drop earthward as if depressed by the weight of its enormous horns; then a dim, white, wavy streak of sheep prolonged itself from that spot in a generally horizontal direction to within about four yards of a point immediately beneath the enemy. There it struck sharply upward, and before it had faded from my gaze at the place whence it had set out I heard a horrid thump and a piercing scream, and my poor uncle shot forward, with a slack rope higher than the limb to which he was attached. Here the rope tautened with a jerk, arresting his flight, and back he swung in a breathless curve to the other end of his arc. The ram had fallen, a heap of indistinguishable legs, wool and horns, but pulling itself together and dodging as its antagonist swept downward it retired at random, alternately shaking its head and stamping its fore-feet. When it had backed about the same distance as that from which it had delivered the assault it paused again, bowed its head as if in prayer for victory and again shot forward, dimly visible as before—a prolonging white streak with monstrous undulations, ending with a sharp ascension. Its course this time was at a right angle to its former one, and its impatience so great that it struck the enemy before he had nearly reached the lowest point of his arc. In consequence he went flying round and round in a horizontal circle whose radius was about equal to half the length of the rope, which I forgot to say was nearly twenty feet long. His shrieks, *crescendo* in approach and *diminuendo* in recession, made the rapidity of his revolution more obvious to the ear than to the eye. He had evidently not yet been struck in a vital spot. His posture in the sack and the distance from the ground at which he hung compelled the ram to operate upon his lower extremities and the end of his back. Like a plant that has struck its root into some poisonous mineral, my poor uncle was dying slowly upward.

"After delivering its second blow the ram had not again retired. The fever of battle burned hot in its heart; its brain was intoxicated with the wine of strife. Like a pugilist who in his rage forgets his skill and fights ineffectively at half-arm's length, the angry beast endeavored to reach its fleeting foe by awkward vertical leaps as he passed overhead, sometimes, indeed, succeeding in striking him feebly, but more frequently overthrown by its own misguided eagerness. But as the impetus was exhausted and the man's circles narrowed in scope and diminished in speed, bringing him nearer to the ground, these tactics produced better results, eliciting a superior quality of screams, which I greatly enjoyed.

"Suddenly, as if the bugles had sung truce, the ram suspended hostilities and walked away, thoughtfully wrinkling and smoothing its great aquiline nose, and occasionally cropping a bunch of grass and slowly munching it. It seemed to have tired of war's alarms and resolved to beat the sword into a plowshare and cultivate the arts of peace. Steadily it held its course away from the field of fame until it had gained a distance of nearly a quarter of a mile. There it stopped and stood with its rear to the foe, chewing its cud and apparently half asleep. I observed, however, an occasional slight turn of its head, as if its apathy were more affected than real.

"Meantime Uncle William's shrieks had abated with his motion, and nothing was heard from him but long, low moans, and at long intervals my name, uttered in pleading tones exceedingly grateful to my ear. Evidently the man had not the faintest notion of what was being done to him, and was inexpressibly terrified. When Death comes cloaked in mystery he is terrible indeed. Little by little my uncle's oscillations diminished, and finally he hung motionless. I went to him and was about to give him the *coup de grâce*, when I heard and felt a succession of smart shocks which shook the ground like a series of light earthquakes, and turning in the direction of the ram, saw a long cloud of dust approaching me with inconceivable rapidity and alarming effect! At a distance of some thirty yards away it stopped short, and from the near end of it rose into the air what I at first thought a great white bird. Its ascent was so smooth and easy and regular that I could not realize its extraordinary celerity, and was lost in admiration of its grace. To this day the impression remains that it was a slow, deliberate movement, the ram—for it was that animal—being upborne by some power other than its own impetus, and supported through the successive stages of its flight with infinite tenderness and care. My eyes followed its progress through the air with unspeakable pleasure, all the greater by contrast with my former terror of its approach by land. Onward and upward the noble animal sailed, its head bent down almost between its knees, its fore-feet thrown back, its hinder legs trailing to rear like the legs of a soaring heron.

"At a height of forty or fifty feet, as fond recollection presents it to view, it attained its zenith and appeared to remain an instant stationary; then, tilting suddenly forward without altering the relative position of its parts, it shot downward on a steeper and steeper course with augmenting velocity, passed immediately above me with a noise like the rush of a cannon shot and struck my poor uncle almost squarely on the top of the head! So frightful was the impact that not only the man's neck was broken, but the rope too; and the body of the deceased, forced against the earth, was crushed to pulp beneath the awful front of that meteoric sheep! The concussion stopped all the clocks between Lone Hand and Dutch Dan's, and Professor Davidson, a distinguished authority in matters seismic, who happened to be in the vicinity, promptly explained that the vibrations were from north to southwest.

"Altogether, I cannot help thinking that in point of artistic atrocity my murder of Uncle William has seldom been excelled."

OIL OF DOG

My name is Boffer Bings. I was born of honest parents in one of the humbler walks of life, my father being a manufacturer of dog-oil and my mother having a small studio in the shadow of the village church, where she disposed of unwelcome babes. In my boyhood I was trained to habits of industry; I not only assisted my father in procuring dogs for his vats, but was frequently employed by my mother to carry away the debris of her work in the studio. In performance of this duty I sometimes had need of all my natural intelligence for all the law officers of the vicinity were opposed to my mother's business. They were not elected on an opposition ticket, and the matter had never been made a political issue; it just happened so. My father's business of making dog-oil was, naturally, less unpopular, though the owners of missing dogs sometimes regarded him with suspicion, which was reflected, to some extent, upon me. My father had, as silent partners, all the physicians of the town, who seldom wrote a prescription which did not contain what they were pleased to designate as *Ol. can.* It is really the most valuable medicine ever discovered. But most persons are unwilling to make personal sacrifices for the afflicted, and it was evident that many of the fattest dogs in town had been forbidden to play with me—a fact which pained my young sensibilities, and at one time came near driving me to become a pirate.

Looking back upon those days, I cannot but regret, at times, that by indirectly bringing my beloved parents to their death I was the author of misfortunes profoundly affecting my future.

One evening while passing my father's oil factory with the body of a foundling from my mother's studio I saw a constable who seemed to be closely watching my movements. Young as I was, I had learned that a constable's acts, of whatever apparent character, are prompted by the most reprehensible motives, and I avoided him by dodging into the oilery by a side door which happened to stand ajar. I locked it at once and was alone with my dead. My father had retired for the night. The only light in the place came from the furnace, which glowed a deep, rich crimson under one of the vats, casting ruddy reflections on the walls. Within the cauldron the oil still rolled in indolent ebullition, occasionally pushing to the surface a piece of dog. Seating myself to wait for the constable to go away, I held the naked body of the foundling in my lap and tenderly stroked its short, silken hair. Ah, how beautiful it was! Even at that early age I was passionately fond of children, and as I looked upon this cherub I could almost find it in my heart to wish that the small, red wound upon its breast—the work of my dear mother—had not been mortal.

It had been my custom to throw the babes into the river which nature had thoughtfully provided for the purpose, but that night I did not dare to leave the oilery for fear of the constable. "After all," I said to myself, "it cannot greatly matter if I put it into this cauldron. My father will never know the bones from those of a puppy, and the few deaths which may result from administering another kind of oil for the incomparable *Ol. can.* are not important in a population which increases so rapidly." In short, I took the first step in crime and brought myself untold sorrow by casting the babe into the cauldron.

The next day, somewhat to my surprise, my father, rubbing his hands with satisfaction, informed me and my mother that he had obtained the finest quality of oil that was ever seen; that the physicians to whom he had shown samples had so pronounced it. He added that he had no knowledge as to how the result was obtained; the dogs had been treated in all respects as usual, and were of an ordinary breed. I deemed it my duty to explain—which I did, though palsied would have been my tongue if I could have foreseen the consequences. Bewailing their previous ignorance of the advantages of combining their industries, my parents at once took measures to repair the error. My mother removed her studio to a wing of the factory building and my duties in connection with the business ceased; I was no longer required to dispose of the bodies of the small superfluous, and there was no need of alluring dogs to their doom, for my father discarded them altogether, though they still had an honorable place in the name of the oil. So suddenly thrown into idleness, I might naturally have been expected to become vicious and dissolute, but I did not. The holy influence of my dear mother was ever about me to protect me from the temptations which beset youth, and my father was a deacon in a church. Alas, that through my fault these estimable persons should have come to so bad an end!

Finding a double profit in her business, my mother now devoted herself to it with a new assiduity. She removed not only superfluous and unwelcome babes to order, but went out into the highways and byways, gathering in children of a larger growth, and even such adults as she could entice to the oilery. My father, too, enamored of the superior quality of oil produced, purveyed for his vats with diligence and zeal. The conversion of their neighbors into dog-oil became, in short, the one passion of their lives—an absorbing and overwhelming greed took possession of their souls and served them in place of a hope in Heaven—by which, also, they were inspired.

So enterprising had they now become that a public meeting was held and resolutions passed severely censuring them. It was intimated by the chairman that any further raids upon the population would be met in a spirit of hostility. My poor parents left the meeting broken-hearted, desperate and, I believe, not altogether sane. Anyhow, I deemed it prudent not to enter the oilery with them that night, but slept outside in a stable.

At about midnight some mysterious impulse caused me to rise and peer through a window into the furnace-room, where I knew my father now slept. The fires were burning as brightly as if the following day's harvest had been expected to be abundant. One of the large cauldrons was slowly "walloping" with a mysterious appearance of self-restraint, as if it bided its time to put forth its full energy. My father was not in bed; he had risen in his night clothes and was preparing a noose in a strong cord. From the looks which the unfriendly action of the citizens and my absence too well the purpose that he had in mind. Speechless and motionless with terror, I could do nothing in prevention or warning. Suddenly the door of my mother's apartment was opened, noiselessly, and the two confronted each other, both apparently surprised. The lady, also, was in her night clothes, and she held in her right hand the tool of her trade, a long, narrow-bladed dagger.

She, too, had been unable to deny herself the last profit which the unfriendly action of the citizens and my absence had left her. For one instant they looked into each other's blazing eyes and then sprang together with indescribable fury. Round and round the room they struggled, the man cursing, the woman shrieking, both fighting like demons— she to strike him with the dagger, he to strangle her with his great bare hands. I know not how long I had the unhappiness to observe this disagreeable instance of domestic infelicity, but at last, after a more than usually vigorous struggle, the combatants suddenly moved apart.

My father's breast and my mother's weapon showed evidences of contact. For another instant they glared at each other in the most unamiable way; then my poor, wounded father, feeling the hand of death upon him, leaped forward, unmindful of resistance, grasped by dear mother in his arms, dragged her to the side of the boiling cauldron, collected all his failing energies, and sprang in with her! In a moment, both had disappeared and were adding their oil to that of the committee of citizens who had called the day before with an invitation to the public meeting.

Convinced that these unhappy events closed to me every avenue to an honorable career in that town, I removed to the famous city of Otumwee, where these memoirs are written with a heart full of remorse for a heedless act entailing so dismal a commercial disaster.

AN IMPERFECT CONFLAGRATION

Early one June morning in 1872 I murdered my father— an act which made a deep impression on me at the time. This was before my marriage, while I was living with my parents in Wisconsin. My father and I were in the library of our home, dividing the proceeds of a burglary which we had committed that night. These consisted of household goods mostly, and the task of equitable division was difficult. We got on very well with the napkins, towels and such things, and the silverware was parted pretty nearly equally, but you can see for yourself that when you try to divide a single music-box by two without a remainder you will have trouble. It was that music-box which brought disaster and disgrace upon our family. If we had left it my poor father might now be alive.

It was a most exquisite and beautiful piece of workman-ship—inlaid with costly woods and carven very curiously. It would not only play a great variety of tunes, but would whistle like a quail, bark like a dog, crow every morning at daylight whether it was wound up or not, and break the Ten Commandments. It was this last mentioned accomplishment that won my father's heart and caused him to commit the only dishonorable act of his life, though possibly he would have committed more if he had been spared: he tried to conceal that music-box from me, and declared upon his honor that he had not taken it, though I knew very well that, so far as he was concerned, the burglary had been under-taken chiefly for the purpose of obtaining it.

My father had the music-box hidden under his cloak; we

had worn cloaks by way of disguise. He had solemnly assured me that he did not take it. I knew that he did, and knew something of which he was evidently ignorant; namely, that the box would crow at daylight and betray him if I could prolong the division of profits till that time. All occurred as I wished: as the gaslight began to pale in the library and the shape of the windows was seen dimly behind the curtains, a long cock-a-doodle-doo came from beneath the old gentleman's cloak, followed by a few bars of an aria from *Tannhäuser,* ending with a loud click. A small hand-axe, which we had used to break into the unlucky house, lay between us on the table; I picked it up. The old man, seeing that further concealment was useless, took the box from under his cloak and set it on the table. "Cut it in two if you prefer that plan," said he; "I tried to save it from destruction."

He was a passionate lover of music and could himself play the concertina with expression and feeling.

I said: "I do not question the purity of your motive: it would be presumptuous in me to sit in judgment on my father. But business is business, and with this axe I am going to effect a dissolution of our partnership unless you will consent in all future burglaries to wear a bell-punch."

"No," he said, after some reflection, "no, I could not do that; it would look like a confession of dishonesty. People would say that you distrusted me."

I could not help admiring his spirit and sensitiveness; for a moment I was proud of him and disposed to overlook his fault, but a glance at the richly jeweled music-box decided me, and, as I said, I removed the old man from this vale of tears. Having done so, I was a trifle uneasy. Not only was he my father—the author of my being—but the body would be certainly discovered. It was now broad daylight and my mother was likely to enter the library at any moment. Under the circumstances, I thought it expedient to remove her also, which I did. Then I paid off all the servants and discharged them.

That afternoon I went to the chief of police, told him what I had done and asked his advice. It would be very painful to me if the facts became publicly known. My conduct would be generally condemned; the newspapers would bring it up against me if ever I should run for office. The chief saw the force of these considerations; he was himself an assassin of wide experience. After consulting with the presiding judge of the Court of Variable Jurisdiction he advised me to conceal the bodies in one of the book-cases, get a heavy insurance on the house and burn it down. This I proceeded to do.

In the library was a book-case which my father had recently purchased of some cranky inventor and had not filled. It was in shape and size something like the old-fashioned "wardrobes" which one sees in bed-rooms without closets, but opened all the way down, like a woman's night-dress. It had glass doors. I had recently laid out my parents and they were now rigid enough to stand erect; so I stood them in this book-case, from which I had removed the shelves. I locked them in and tacked some curtains over the glass doors. The inspector from the insurance office passed a half-dozen times before the case without suspicion.

That night, after getting my policy, I set fire to the house and started through the woods to town, two miles away, where I managed to be found about the time the excitement was at its height. With cries of apprehension for the fate of my parents, I joined the rush and arrived at the fire some two hours after I had kindled it. The whole town was there as I dashed up. The house was entirely consumed, but in one end of the level bed of glowing embers, bolt upright and uninjured, was that book-case! The curtains had burned away, exposing the glass-doors, through which the fierce, red light illuminated the interior. There stood my dear father "in his habit as he lived," and at his side the partner of his joys and sorrows. Not a hair of them was singed, their clothing was intact. On their heads and throats the injuries which in the accomplishment of my designs I had been compelled to inflict were conspicuous. As in the presence of a miracle, the people were silent; awe and terror had stilled every tongue. I was myself greatly affected.

Some three years later, when the events herein related had nearly faded from my memory, I went to New York to assist in passing some counterfeit United States bonds. Carelessly looking into a furniture store one day, I saw the exact counterpart of that book-case. "I bought it for a trifle from a reformed inventor," the dealer explained. "He said it was fireproof, the pores of the wood being filled with alum under hydraulic pressure and the glass made of asbestos. I don't suppose it is really fireproof—you can have it at the price of an ordinary book-case."

"No," I said, "if you cannot warrant it fireproof I won't take it"—and I bade him good morning.

I would not have had it at any price: it revived memories that were exceedingly disagreeable.

THE HYPNOTIST

By those of my friends who happen to know that I sometimes amuse myself with hypnotism, mind reading and kindred phenomena, I am frequently asked if I have a clear conception of the nature of whatever principle underlies them. To this question I always reply that I neither have nor desire to have. I am no investigator with an ear at the keyhole of Nature's workshop, trying with vulgar curiosity to steal the secrets of her trade. The interests of science are as little to me as mine seem to have been to science.

Doubtless the phenomena in question are simple enough, and in no way transcend our powers of comprehension if only we could find the clew; but for my part I prefer not to find it, for I am of a singularly romantic disposition, deriving more gratification from mystery than from knowledge. It was commonly remarked of me when I was a child that my big blue eyes appeared to have been made rather to look into than look out of—such was their dreamful beauty, and in my frequent periods of abstraction, their indifference to what was going on. In those peculiarities they resembled, I venture to think, the soul which lies behind them, always more intent upon some lovely conception which it has created in its own image than concerned about the laws of nature and the material frame of things. All this, irrelevant and egotistic as it may seem, is related by way of accounting for the meagreness of the light that I am able to throw upon a subject that has engaged so much of my attention, and concerning which there is so keen and general a curiosity. With my powers and opportunities, another person might doubtless have an explanation for much of what I present simply as narrative.

My first knowledge that I possessed unusual powers came to me in my fourteenth year, when at school. Happening one day to have forgotten to bring my noon-day luncheon, I gazed longingly at that of a small girl who was preparing to eat hers. Looking up, her eyes met mine and she seemed unable to withdraw them. After a moment of hesitancy she came forward in an absent kind of way and without a word surrendered her little basket with its tempting contents and walked away. Inexpressibly pleased, I relieved my hunger and destroyed the basket. After that I had not the trouble to bring a luncheon for myself: that little girl was my daily purveyor; and not infrequently in satisfying my simple need from her frugal store I combined pleasure and profit by constraining her attendance at the feast and making misleading proffer of the viands, which eventually I consumed to the last fragment. The girl was always persuaded that she had eaten all herself; and later in the day her tearful complaints of hunger surprised the teacher, entertained the pupils, earned for her the sobriquet of Greedy-Gut and filled me with a peace past understanding.

A disagreeable feature of this otherwise satisfactory condition of things was the necessary secrecy: the transfer of the luncheon, for example, had to be made at some distance from the madding crowd, in a wood; and I blush to think of the many other unworthy subterfuges entailed by the situation. As I was (and am) naturally of a frank and open disposition, these became more and more irksome, and but for the reluctance of my parents to renounce the obvious advantages of the new *régime* I would gladly have reverted to the old. The plan that I finally adopted to free myself from the consequences of my own powers excited a wide and keen interest at the time, and that part of it which consisted in the death of the girl was severely condemned, but it is hardly pertinent to the scope of this narrative.

For some years afterward I had little opportunity to

practice hypnotism; such small essays as I made at it were commonly barren of other recognition than solitary confinement on a bread-and-water diet; sometimes, indeed, they elicited nothing better than the cat-o'-nine-tails. It was when I was about to leave the scene of these small disappointments that my one really important feat was performed.

I had been called into the warden's office and given a suit of civilian's clothing, a trifling sum of money and a great deal of advice, which I am bound to confess was of a much better quality than the clothing. As I was passing out of the gate into the light of freedom I suddenly turned and looking the warden gravely in the eye, soon had him in control.

"You are an ostrich," I said.

At the post-mortem examination the stomach was found to contain a great quantity of indigestible articles mostly of wood or metal. Stuck fast in the œsophagus and constituting, according to the Coroner's jury, the immediate cause of death, one door-knob.

I was by nature a good and affectionate son, but as I took my way into the great world from which I had been so long secluded I could not help remembering that all my misfortunes had flowed like a stream from the niggard economy of my parents in the matter of school luncheons; and I knew of no reason to think they had reformed.

On the road between Succotash Hill and South Asphyxia is a little open field which once contained a shanty known as Pete Gilstrap's Place, where that gentleman used to murder travelers for a living. The death of Mr. Gilstrap and the diversion of nearly all the travel to another road occurred so nearly at the same time that no one has ever been able to say which was cause and which effect. Anyhow, the field was now a desolation and the Place had long been burned. It was while going afoot to South Asphyxia, the home of my childhood, that I found both my parents on their way to the Hill. They had hitched their team and were eating luncheon under an oak tree in the center of the field. The sight of the luncheon called up painful memories of my school days and roused the sleeping lion in my breast. Approaching the guilty couple, who at once recognized me, I ventured to suggest that I share their hospitality.

"Of this cheer, my son," said the author of my being, with characteristic pomposity, which age had not withered, "there is sufficient for but two. I am not, I hope, insensible to the hunger-light in your eyes, but—"

My father has never completed that sentence; what he mistook for hunger-light was simply the earnest gaze of the hypnotist. In a few seconds he was at my service. A few more sufficed for the lady, and the dictates of a just resentment could be carried into effect. "My former father," I said, "I presume that it is known to you that you and this lady are no longer what you were?"

"I have observed a certain subtle change," was the rather dubious reply of the old gentleman; "it is perhaps attributable to age."

"It is more than that," I explained; "it goes to character— to species. You and the lady here are, in truth, two *broncos*— wild stallions both, and unfriendly."

"Why, John," exclaimed my dear mother, "you don't mean to say that I am—"

"Madam," I replied, solemnly, fixing my eyes again upon hers, "you are."

Scarcely had the words fallen from my lips when she dropped upon her hands and knees, and backing up to the old man squealed like a demon and delivered a vicious kick upon his shin! An instant later he was himself down on all-fours, headed away from her and flinging his feet at her simultaneously and successively. With equal earnestness but inferior agility, because of her hampering body-gear, she plied her own. Their flying legs crossed and mingled in the most bewildering way; their feet sometimes meeting squarely in midair, their bodies thrust forward, falling flat upon the ground and for a moment helpless. On recovering themselves they would resume the combat, uttering their frenzy in the nameless sounds of the furious brutes which they believed themselves to be—the whole region rang with their clamor! Round and round they wheeled, the blows of their feet falling "like lightnings from the mountain cloud." They plunged and reared backward upon their knees, struck savagely at each other with awkward descending blows of both fists at once, and dropped again upon their hands as if unable to maintain the upright position of the body. Grass and pebbles were torn from the soil by hands and feet; clothing, hair, faces inexpressibly defiled with dust and blood. Wild, inarticulate screams of rage attested the delivery of the blows; groans, grunts and gasps their receipt. Nothing more truly military was ever seen at Gettysburg or Waterloo: the valor of my dear parents in the hour of danger can never cease to be to me a source of pride and gratification. At the end of it all two battered, tattered, bloody and fragmentary vestiges of mortality attested the solemn fact that the author of the strife was an orphan.

Arrested for provoking a breach of the peace, I was, and have ever since been, tried in the Court of Technicalities and Continuances whence, after fifteen years of proceedings, my attorney is moving heaven and earth to get the case taken to the Court of Remandment for New Trials.

Such are a few of my principal experiments in the mysterious force or agency known as hypnotic suggestion. Whether or not it could be employed by a bad man for an unworthy purpose I am unable to say.

Selection from

THE FOURTH ESTATE

"THE BUBBLE REPUTATION"

HOW ANOTHER MAN'S WAS SOUGHT AND PRICKED

It was a stormy night in the autumn of 1930. The hour was about eleven. San Francisco lay in darkness, for the laborers at the gas works had struck and destroyed the company's property because a newspaper to which a cousin of the manager was a subscriber had censured the course of a potato merchant related by marriage to a member of the Knights of Leisure. Electric lights had not at that period been reinvented. The sky was filled with great masses of black cloud which, driven rapidly across the star-fields by winds unfelt on the earth and momentarily altering their fantastic forms, seemed instinct with a life and activity of their own and endowed with awful powers of evil, to the exercise of which they might at any time set their malignant will.

An observer standing, at this time, at the corner of Paradise avenue and Great White Throne walk in Sorrell Hill cemetery would have seen a human figure moving among the graves toward the Superintendent's residence. Dimly and fitfully visible in the intervals of thinner gloom, this figure had a most uncanny and disquieting aspect. A long black cloak shrouded it from neck to heel. Upon its head was a slouch hat, pulled down across the forehead and almost concealing the face, which was further hidden by a half-mask, only the beard being occasionally visible as the head was lifted partly above the collar of the cloak. The man wore upon his feet jack-boots whose wide, funnel-shaped legs had settled down in many a fold and crease about his ankles, as could be seen whenever accident parted the bottom of the cloak. His arms were concealed, but sometimes he stretched out the right to steady himself by a headstone as he crept stealthily but blindly over the uneven ground. At such times a close scrutiny of the hand would have disclosed in the palm the hilt of a poniard, the blade of which lay along the wrist, hidden in the sleeve. In short, the man's garb, his movements, the hour—everything proclaimed him a reporter.

But what did he there?

On the morning of that day the editor of the *Daily Malefactor* had touched the button of a bell numbered 216 and in response to the summons Mr. Longbo Spittleworth, reporter, had been shot into the room out of an inclined tube.

"I understand," said the editor, "that you are 216—am I right?"

"That," said the reporter, catching his breath and adjusting his clothing, both somewhat disordered by the celerity of his flight through the tube,—"that is my number."

"Information has reached us," continued the editor, "that the Superintendent of the Sorrel Hill cemetery—one Inhumio, whose very name suggests inhumanity—is guilty of the grossest outrages in the administration of the great trust confided to his hands by the sovereign people."

"The cemetery is private property," faintly suggested 216.

"It is alleged," continued the great man, disdaining to notice the interruption, "that in violation of popular rights he refuses to permit his accounts to be inspected by representatives of the press."

"Under the law, you know, he is responsible to the directors of the cemetery company," the reporter ventured to interject.

"They say," pursued the editor, heedless, "that the inmates are in many cases badly lodged and insufficiently clad, and that in consequence they are usually cold. It is asserted that they are never fed—except to the worms. Statements have been made to the effect that males and females are permitted to occupy the same quarters, to the incalculable detriment of public morality. Many clandestine villainies are alleged of this fiend in human shape, and it is desirable that his underground methods be unearthed in the *Malefactor*. If he resists we will drag his family skeleton from the privacy of his domestic closet. There is money in it for the paper, fame for you—are you ambitious, 216?"

"I am—bitious."

"Go, then," cried the editor, rising and waving his hand imperiously—"go and 'seek the bubble reputation.'"

"The bubble shall be sought," the young man replied, and leaping into a man-hole in the floor, disappeared. A moment later the editor, who after dismissing his subordinate, had stood motionless, as if lost in thought, sprang suddenly to the man-hole and shouted down it: "Hello, 216?"

"Aye, aye, sir," came up a faint and far reply.

"About that 'bubble reputation'—you understand, I suppose, that the reputation which you are to seek is that of the other man."

In the execution of his duty, in the hope of his employer's approval, in the costume of his profession, Mr. Longbo Spittleworth, otherwise known as 216, has already occupied a place in the mind's eye of the intelligent reader. Alas for poor Mr. Inhumio!

A few days after these events that fearless, independent and enterprising guardian and guide of the public, the San Francisco *Daily Malefactor,* contained a whole-page article whose headlines are here presented with some necessary typographical mitigation:

"Hell Upon Earth! Corruption Rampant in the Management of the Sorrel Hill Cemetery. The Sacred City of the Dead in the Leprous Clutches of a Demon in Human Form. Fiendish Atrocities Committed in 'God's Acre.' The Holy Dead Thrown around Loose. Fragments of Mothers. Segregation of a Beautiful Young Lady Who in Life Was the Light of a Happy Household. A Superintendent Who Is an Ex-Convict. How He Murdered His Neighbor to Start

the Cemetery. He Buries His Own Dead Elsewhere. Extra-
ordinary Insolence to a Representative of the Public Press.
Little Eliza's Last Words: 'Mamma, Feed Me to the Pigs.'
A Moonshiner Who Runs an Illicit Bone-Button Factory in
One Corner of the Grounds. Buried Head Downward. Re-
volting Mausoleistic Orgies. Dancing on the Dead. Devilish
Mutilation—a Pile of Late Lamented Noses and Sainted
Ears. No Separation of the Sexes; Petition's for Chaperons
Unheeded. 'Veal' as Supplied to the Superintendent's Em-
ployees. A Miscreant's Record from His Birth. Disgusting
Subserviency of Our Contemporaries and Strong Indications
of Collusion. Nameless Abnormalities. 'Doubled Up Like a
Nut-Cracker.' 'Wasn't Planted White.' Horribly Significant
Reduction in the Price of Lard. The Question of the Hour:
Whom Do You Fry Your Doughnuts In?"

THE OCEAN WAVE

A SHIPWRECKOLLECTION

As I left the house she said I was a cruel old thing, and not a bit nice, and she hoped I never, never *would* come back. So I shipped as mate on the *Mudlark,* bound from London to wherever the captain might think it expedient to sail. It had not been thought advisable to hamper Captain Abersouth with orders, for when he could not have his own way, it had been observed, he would contrive in some ingenious way to make the voyage unprofitable. The owners of the *Mudlark* had grown wise in their generation, and now let him do pretty much as he pleased, carrying such cargoes as he fancied to ports where the nicest women were. On the voyage of which I write he had taken no cargo at all; he said it would only make the *Mudlark* heavy and slow. To hear this mariner talk one would have supposed he did not know very much about commerce.

We had a few passengers—not nearly so many as we had laid in basins and stewards for; for before coming off to the ship most of those who had bought tickets would inquire whither she was bound, and when not informed would go back to their hotels and send a bandit on board to remove their baggage. But there were enough left to be rather troublesome. They cultivated the rolling gait peculiar to sailors when drunk, and the upper deck was hardly wide enough for them to go from the forecastle to the binnacle to set their watches by the ship's compass. They were always petitioning Captain Abersouth to let the big anchor go, just to hear it plunge in the water, threatening in case of refusal to write to the newspapers. A favorite amusement with them was to sit in the lee of the bulwarks, relating their experiences in former voyages—voyages distinguished in every instance by two remarkable features, the frequency of unprecedented hurricanes and the entire immunity of the narrator from seasickness. It was very interesting to see them sitting in a row telling these things, each man with a basin between his legs.

One day there arose a great storm. The sea walked over the ship as if it had never seen a ship before and meant to enjoy it all it could. The *Mudlark* labored very much—far more, indeed, than the crew did; for these innocents had discovered in possession of one of their number a pair of leather-seated trousers, and would do nothing but sit and play cards for them; in a month from leaving port each sailor had owned them a dozen times. They were so worn by being pushed over to the winner that there was little but the seat remaining, and that immortal part the captain finally kicked overboard—not maliciously, nor in an unfriendly spirit, but because he had a habit of kicking the seats of trousers.

The storm increased in violence until it succeeded in so straining the *Mudlark* that she took in water like a teetotaler; then it appeared to get relief directly. This may be said in justice to a storm at sea: when it has broken off your masts, pulled out your rudder, carried away your boats and made a nice hole in some inaccessible part of your hull it will often go away in search of a fresh ship, leaving you to take such measures for your comfort as you may think fit. In our case the captain thought fit to sit on the taffrail reading a three-volume novel.

Seeing he had got about half way through the second volume, at which point the lovers would naturally be involved in the most hopeless and heart-rending difficulties, I thought he would be in a particularly cheerful humor, so I approached him and informed him the ship was going down.

"Well," said he, closing the book, but keeping his forefinger between the pages to mark his place, "she never would

be good for much after such a shaking-up as this. But, I say—
I wish you would just send the bo'sn for'd there to break
up that prayer-meeting. The *Mudlark* isn't a seamen's chapel,
I suppose."

"But," I replied, impatiently, "can't something be done
to lighten the ship?"

"Well," he drawled, reflectively, "seeing she hasn't any
masts left to cut away, nor any cargo to—stay, you might
throw over some of the heaviest of the passengers if you
think it would do any good."

It was a happy thought—the intuition of genius. Walking
rapidly forward to the foc'sle, which, being highest out of
water, was crowded with passengers, I seized a stout old
gentleman by the nape of the neck, pushed him up to the
rail, and chucked him over. He did not touch the water:
he fell on the apex of a cone of sharks which sprang up
from the sea to meet him, their noses gathered to a point,
their tails just clearing the surface. I think it unlikely that
the old gentleman knew what disposition had been made of
him. Next, I hurled over a woman and flung a fat baby to
the wild winds. The former was sharked out of sight, the
same as the old man; the latter divided amongst the gulls.

I am relating these things exactly as they occurred. It
would be very easy to make a fine story out of all this
material—to tell how that, while I was engaged in lightening
the ship, I was touched by the self-sacrificing spirit of a
beautiful young woman, who, to save the life of her lover,
pushed her aged mother forward to where I was operating,
imploring me to take the old lady, but spare, O, spare her
dear Henry. I might go on to set forth how that I not only
did take the old lady, as requested, but immediately seized
dear Henry, and sent him flying as far as I could to leeward,
having first broken his back across the rail and pulled a
double-fistful of his curly hair out. I might proceed to state
that, feeling appeased, I then stole the long boat and taking
the beautiful maiden pulled away from the ill-fated ship to
the church of St. Massaker, Fiji, where we were united by
a knot which I afterward untied with my teeth by eating
her. But, in truth, nothing of all this occurred, and I can
not afford to be the first writer to tell a lie just to interest the

reader. What really did occur is this: as I stood on the quarter-deck, heaving over the passengers, one after another, Captain Abersouth, having finished his novel, walked aft and quietly hove *me* over.

The sensations of a drowning man have been so often related that I shall only briefly explain that memory at once displayed her treasures: all the scenes of my eventful life crowded, though without confusion or fighting, into my mind. I saw my whole career spread out before me, like a map of Central Africa since the discovery of the gorilla. There were the cradle in which I had lain, as a child, stupefied with soothing syrups; the perambulator, seated in which and propelled from behind, I overthrew the school-master, and in which my infantile spine received its curvature; the nursery-maid, surrendering her lips alternately to me and the gardener; the old home of my youth, with the ivy and the mortgage on it; my eldest brother, who by will succeeded to the family debts; my sister, who ran away with the Count von Pretzel, coachman to a most respectable New York family; my mother, standing in the attitude of a saint, pressing with both hands her prayer-book against the patent palpitators from Madame Fahertini's; my venerable father, sitting in his chimney corner, his silvered head bowed upon his breast, his withered hands crossed patiently in his lap, waiting with Christian resignation for death, and drunk as a lord—all this, and much more, came before my mind's eye, and there was no charge for admission to the show. Then there was a ringing sound in my ears, my senses swam better than I could, and as I sank down, down, through fathomless depths, the amber light falling through the water above my head failed and darkened into blackness. Suddenly my feet struck something firm—it was the bottom. Thank heaven, I was saved!

THE CAPTAIN OF "THE CAMEL"

This ship was named the *Camel*. In some ways she was an extraordinary vessel. She measured six hundred tons;

but when she had taken in enough ballast to keep her from
upsetting like a shot duck, and was provisioned for a three
months' voyage, it was necessary to be mighty fastidious in
the choice of freight and passengers. For illustration, as she
was about to leave port a boat came alongside with two
passengers, a man and his wife. They had booked the day
before, but had remained ashore to get one more decent
meal before committing themselves to the "briny cheap,"
as the man called the ship's fare. The woman came aboard,
and the man was preparing to follow, when the captain
leaned over the side and saw him.

"Well," said the captain, "what do *you* want?"

"What do *I* want?" said the man, laying hold of the ladder.
"I'm a-going to embark in this here ship—that's what I
want."

"Not with all that fat on you," roared the captain. "You
don't weigh an ounce less than eighteen stone, and I've got
to have in my anchor yet. You wouldn't have me leave the
anchor, I suppose?"

The man said he did not care about the anchor—he was
just as God had made him (he looked as if his cook had had
something to do with it) and, sink or swim, he purposed
embarking in that ship. A good deal of wrangling ensued,
but one of the sailors finally threw the man a cork life-pre-
server, and the captain said that would lighten him and he
might come aboard.

This was Captain Abersouth, formerly of the *Mudlark*—
as good a seaman as ever sat on the taffrail reading a three-
volume novel. Nothing could equal this man's passion for
literature. For every voyage he laid in so many bales of
novels that there was no stowage for the cargo. There were
novels in the hold, and novels between-decks, and novels in
the saloon, and in the passengers' beds.

The *Camel* had been designed and built by her owner,
an architect in the City, and she looked about as much like
a ship as Noah's Ark did. She had bay windows and a ver-
anda; a cornice and doors at the waterline. These doors had
knockers and servant's bells. There had been a futile attempt at an area. The passenger saloon was on the upper
deck, and had a tile roof. To this humplike structure the

ship owed her name. Her designer had erected several churches—that of St. Ignotus is still used as a brewery in Hotbath Meadows—and, possessed of the ecclesiastic idea, had given the *Camel* a transept; but, finding this impeded her passage through the water, he had it removed. This weakened the vessel amidships. The mainmast was something like a steeple. It had a weathercock. From this spire the eye commanded one of the finest views in England.

Such was the *Camel* when I joined her in 1864 for a voyage of discovery to the South Pole. The expedition was under the "auspices" of the Royal Society for the Promotion of Fair Play. At a meeting of this excellent association, it had been "resolved" that the partiality of science for the North Pole was an invidious distinction between two objects equally meritorious; that Nature had marked her disapproval of it in the case of Sir John Franklin and many of his imitators; that it served them very well right; that this enterprise should be undertaken as a protest against the spirit of undue bias; and, finally, that no part of the responsibility or expense should devolve upon the society in its corporate character, but any individual member might contribute to the fund if he were fool enough. It is only common justice to say that none of them was. The *Camel* merely parted her cable one day while I happened to be on board— drifted out of the harbor southward, followed by the execrations of all who knew her, and could not get back. In two months she had crossed the equator, and the heat began to grow insupportable.

Suddenly we were becalmed. There had been a fine breeze up to three o'clock in the afternoon and the ship had made as much as two knots an hour when without a word of warning the sails began to belly the wrong way, owing to the impetus that the ship had acquired; and then, as this expired, they hung as limp and lifeless as the skirts of a claw-hammer coat. The *Camel* not only stood stock still but moved a little backward toward England. Old Ben the boatswain said that he'd never knowed but one deader calm, and that, he explained, was when Preacher Jack, the reformed sailor, had got excited in a sermon in a seaman's chapel and shouted that the Archangel Michael would chuck the Dragon into the brig and give him a taste of the rope's-end, damn his eyes!

We lay in this woful state for the better part of a year, when, growing impatient, the crew deputed me to look up the captain and see if something could not be done about it. I found him in a remote cobwebby corner between-decks, with a book in his hand. On one side of him, the cords newly cut, were three bales of "Ouida"; on the other a mountain of Miss M. E. Braddon towered above his head. He had finished "Ouida" and was tackling Miss Braddon. He was greatly changed.

"Captain Abersouth," said I, rising on tiptoe so as to over-look the lower slopes of Mrs. Braddon, "will you be good enough to tell me how long this thing is going on?"

"Can't say, I'm sure," he replied without pulling his eyes off the page. "They'll probably make up about the middle of the book. In the meantime old Pondronummus will foul his top-hamper and take out his papers for Looney Haven, and young Monshure de Boojower will come in for a mil-lion. Then if the proud and fair Angelica doesn't luff and come into his wake after pizening that sea lawyer, Thunder-muzzle, I don't know nothing about the deeps and shallers of the human heart."

I could not take so hopeful a view of the situation, and went on deck, feeling very much discouraged. I had no sooner got my head out than I observed that the ship was moving at a high rate of speed!

We had on board a bullock and a Dutchman. The bullock was chained by the neck to the foremast, but the Dutchman was allowed a good deal of liberty, being shut up at night only. There was bad blood between the two—a feud of long standing, having its origin in the Dutchman's appetite for milk and the bullock's sense of personal dignity; the par-ticular cause of offense it would be tedious to relate. Taking advantage of his enemy's afternoon *siesta,* the Dutchman had now managed to sneak by him, and had gone out on the bowsprit to fish. When the animal waked and saw the other creature enjoying himself he straddled his chain, leveled his horns, got his hind feet against the mast and laid a course for the offender. The chain was strong, the mast firm, and the ship, as Byron says, "walked the water like a thing of course."

After that we kept the Dutchman right where he was, night and day, the old *Camel* making better speed than she had ever done in the most favorable gale. We held due south.

We had now been a long time without sufficient food, particularly meat. We could spare neither the bullock nor the Dutchman; and the ship's carpenter, that traditional first aid to the famished, was a mere bag of bones. The fish would neither bite nor be bitten. Most of the running-tackle of the ship had been used for macaroni soup; all the leather work, our shoes included, had been devoured in omelettes; with oakum and tar we had made fairly supportable salad. After a brief experimental career as tripe the sails had departed this life forever. Only two courses remained from which to choose; we could eat one another, as is the etiquette of the sea, or partake of Captain Abersouth's novels. Dreadful alternative!—but a choice. And it is seldom, I think, that starving sailormen are offered a shipload of the best popular authors ready-roasted by the critics.

We ate that fiction. The works that the captain had thrown aside lasted six months, for most of them were by the best-selling authors and were pretty tough. After they were gone—of course some had to be given to the bullock and the Dutchman—we stood by the captain, taking the other books from his hands as he finished them. Sometimes, when we were apparently at our last gasp, he would skip a whole page of moralizing, or a bit of description; and always, as soon as he clearly foresaw the *dénoûment*—which he generally did at about the middle of the second volume— the work was handed over to us without a word of repining.

The effect of this diet was not unpleasant but remarkable. Physically, it sustained us; mentally, it exalted us; morally, it made us but a trifle worse than we were. We talked as no human beings ever talked before. Our wit was polished but without point. As in a stage broadsword combat, every cut has its parry, so in our conversation every remark suggested the reply, and this necessitated a certain rejoinder. The sequence once interrupted, the whole was bosh; when the thread was broken the beads were seen to be waxen and hollow.

We made love to one another, and plotted darkly in the deepest obscurity of the hold. Each set of conspirators had its proper listener at the hatch. These, leaning too far over would bump their heads together and fight. Occasionally there was confusion amongst them: two or more would assert a right to overhear the same plot. I remember at one time the cook, the carpenter, the second assistant-surgeon, and an able seaman contended with handspikes for the honor of betraying my confidence. Once there were three masked murderers of the second watch bending at the same instant over the sleeping form of a cabin-boy, who had been heard to mutter, a week previously, that he had "Gold! gold!" the accumulation of eighty—yes, eighty—years' piracy on the high seas, while sitting as M.P. for the borough of Zaccheus-cum-Down, and attending church regularly. I saw the captain of the foretop surrounded by suitors for his hand, while he was himself fingering the edge of a packing-case, and singing an amorous ditty to a lady-love shaving at a mirror.

Our diction consisted, in about equal parts, of classical allusion, quotation from the stable, simper from the scullery, cant from the clubs, and the technical slang of heraldry. We boasted much of ancestry, and admired the whiteness of our hands whenever the skin was visible through a fault in the grease and tar. Next to love, the vegetable kingdom, murder, arson, adultery and ritual, we talked most of art. The wooden figure-head of the *Camel,* representing a Guinea nigger detecting a bad smell, and the monochrome picture of two back-broken dolphins on the stern, acquired a new importance. The Dutchman had destroyed the nose of the one by kicking his toes against it, and the other was nearly obliterated by the slops of the cook; but each had its daily pilgrimage, and each constantly developed occult beauties of design and subtle excellences of execution. On the whole we were greatly altered; and if the supply of contemporary fiction had been equal to the demand, the *Camel,* I fear, would not have been strong enough to contain the moral and æsthetic forces fired by the maceration of the brains of authors in the gastric juices of sailors.

Having now got the ship's literature off his mind into ours, the captain went on deck for the first time since leaving port. We were still steering the same course, and, taking his first observation of the sun, the captain discovered that we were in latitude 83° south. The heat was insufferable; the air was like the breath of a furnace within a furnace. The sea steamed like a boiling cauldron, and in the vapor our bodies were temptingly parboiled—our ultimate meal was preparing. Warped by the sun, the ship held both ends high out of the water; the deck of the forecastle was an inclined plane, on which the bullock labored at a disadvantage; but the bowsprit was now vertical and the Dutchman's tenure precarious. A thermometer hung against the mainmast, and we grouped ourselves about it as the captain went up to examine the register.

"One hundred and ninety degrees Fahrenheit!" he muttered in evident astonishment. "Impossible!" Turning sharply about, he ran his eyes over us, and inquired in a peremptory tone, "who's been in command while I was runnin' my eye over that book?"

"Well, captain," I replied, as respectfully as I knew how, "the fourth day out I had the unhappiness to be drawn into a dispute about a game of cards with your first and second officers. In the absence of those excellent seamen, sir, I thought it my duty to assume control of the ship."

"Killed 'em, hey?"

"Sir, they committed suicide by questioning the efficacy of four kings and an ace."

"Well, you lubber, what have you to say in defense of this extraordinary weather?"

"Sir, it is no fault of mine. We are far—very far south, and it is now the middle of July. The weather is uncomfortable, I admit; but considering the latitude and season, it is not, I protest, unseasonable."

"Latitude and season!" he shrieked, livid with rage— "latitude and season! Why, you junk-rigged, flat-bottomed, meadow lugger, don't you know any better than that? Didn't yer little baby brother ever tell ye that southern latitudes is colder than northern, and that July is the middle o' winter here? Go below, you son of a scullion, or I'll break your bones!"

"Oh! very well," I replied; "I'm not going to stay on deck and listen to such low language as that, I warn you. Have it your own way."

The words had no sooner left my lips, than a piercing cold wind caused me to cast my eye upon the thermometer. In the new régime of science the mercury was descending rapidly; but in a moment the instrument was obscured by a blinding fall of snow. Towering icebergs rose from the water on every side, hanging their jagged masses hundreds of feet above the masthead, and shutting us completely in. The ship twisted and writhed; her decks bulged upward, and every timber groaned and cracked like the report of a pistol. The *Camel* was frozen fast. The jerk of her sudden stopping snapped the bullock's chain, and sent both that animal and the Dutchman over the bows, to accomplish their warfare on the ice.

Elbowing my way forward to go below, as I had threatened, I saw the crew tumble to the deck on either hand like ten-pins. They were frozen stiff. Passing the captain, I asked him sneeringly how he liked the weather under the new régime. He replied with a vacant stare. The chill had penetrated to the brain, and affected his mind. He murmured:

"In this delightful spot, happy in the world's esteem, and surrounded by all that makes existence dear, they passed the remainder of their lives. The End."

His jaw dropped. The captain of the *Camel* was dead.

Selections from

TANGENTIAL VIEWS

GEORGE THE MADE-OVER

The English have a distinctly higher and better opinion of Washington than is held in this country. Washington, if he could have a choice in the matter, would indubitably prefer his position in the minds of educated Englishmen to the one that he holds "in the hearts of his countrymen"— not the one that he is said to hold. The superior validity of the English view is due to the better view-point. It is remote, as the American will be when several more generations shall have passed and Americans are devoid (as Englishmen are devoid now) of passions and prejudices engendered in the heat of our "Revolution." We should remember that it was not to the English a revolution, but a small and distant squabble, which cut no great figure in the larger affairs in which they were engaged; and the very memory of it was nearly effaced in that of the next generation by the stupendous events of the French Revolution and the Napoleonic wars. To ears filled with the thunders of Waterloo, the crepitating echoes of the spat at Bunker Hill were inaudible.

No benign personage in the calendar of secular saints is really less loved than Washington. The romancing historians and biographers have adorned him with a thousand impossible virtues, naturally, and in so dehumanizing him have set him beyond and above the longest reach of human sympathies. His character, as it pleased them to create it, is like nothing that we know about and care for. He is a monster of goodness and wisdom, with about as much of light and fire as the snow Adam of the small boy playing at creation on the campus of a public school. The Washington-making Frankensteins have done their work so badly that their creature is an insupportable bore, diffusing an infectious dejection. Try to fancy an historical novel or drama with him for hero—a poem with him for subject! Possibly such have been written; I do not recall any at the moment, and the proposition is hardly thinkable. The ideal Washington is a soulless conception, absolutely without power on the imagination. Within the area of his gelid efflation the flowers of fancy open only to wither, and any sentiment endeavoring to transgress the boundary of that desolate domain falls frosted in its flight.

Some one—Colonel Ingersoll, I fancy—has said that Washington is a steel engraving. That is hardly an adequate conception, being derived from the sense of sight only; the ear has something to say in the matter, and there is much in a name. Before my studies of his character had effaced my childish impression I used always to picture him in the act of bending over a tub.

There are two George Washingtons—the natural and the artificial. They are now equally "great," but the former was choke-full of the old Adam. He swore like "our army in Flanders," loved a bottle like a brother and had an intercolonial reputation as a lady-killer. He was, indeed, a singularly interesting and magnetic old boy—one whom any sane and honest lover of the picturesque in life and character would deem it an honor and an education to have known in the flesh. He is now known to but few; you must dig pretty deeply into the tumulus of rubbishy panegyric—scan pretty closely the inedited annals of his time, in order to see him as he was. Criss-crossed upon these failing parchments of the past are the lines of the sleek Philistine, the smug patriot and the lessoning moraler, making a palimpsest whereof all that is legible is false and all that is honest is blotted out. The detestable anthropolater of the biographical gift has pushed his glowing pen across the page, to the unspeakable darkening of counsel. In short, Washington's countrymen see him through a glass dirtily. The image is unlovely and unloved. You can no more love and revere the memory of the biographical George Washington than you can an isosceles triangle or a cubic foot of interstellar space.

The portrait-painters began it—Gilbert Stuart and the rest of them. They idealized all the humanity out of the poor patriot's face and passed him down to the engravers as a rather sleepy-looking butcher's block. There is not a portrait of Washington extant which a man of taste and knowledge would suffer to hang on the wall of his stable. Then the historians jumped in, raping all the laurels from the brows of the man's great contemporaries and piling them in confusion upon his pate. They made him a god in wisdom, and a giant in arms; whereas, in point of ability and service, he was but little, if at all, superior to any one of a half-dozen of his now over-shadowed but once illustrious co-workers in council and camp, and in no way comparable with Hamilton. He towers above his fellows because he stands upon a pile of books.

The supreme indignity to the memory of this really worthy man has been performed by the Sunday-scholiasts, the pietaries, the truly good, the example-to-American-youth folk. These canting creatures have managed to nake him of his last remaining rag of flesh and drain out his ultimate red corpuscle of human blood. In order that he may be acceptable to themselves they have made him a bore to everyone else. To give him value as an "example" to the unripe intelligences of their following they have whitewashed him an inch thick, draped him, fig-leafed him and gilded him out of all semblance to man. To prepare his character for the juvenile moral tooth they have boned it, and to make it digestible to the juvenile moral paunch, unsalted it by maceration in the milk-and-water of their own minds. And so we have him to-day. In a single century the great-hearted gentleman of history has become the good boy of literature —the public prig. Washington is the capon of our barnyard Pantheon—revised and edited for the table.

COLUMBUS

The human mind is affected with a singular disability to get a sense of an historical event without a gigantic figure in the foreground overtopping all his fellows. As surely as God liveth, if one hundred congenital idiots were set adrift in a scow to get rid of them, and, borne by favoring currents into eyeshot of an unknown continent, should simultaneously shout, "Land ho!" instantly drowning in their owl drool, we should have one of them figuring in history ever thereafter with a growing glory as an illustrious discoverer of his time. I do not say that Columbus was a navigator and discoverer of that kind, nor that he did anything of that kind in that way; the parallel is perfect only in what history has done to Columbus; and some seventy millions of Americans are authenticating the imposture all they know how. In this whole black business hardly one element of falsehood is lacking.

Columbus was not a learned man, but an ignorant. He was not an honorable man, but a professional pirate. He was, in the most hateful sense of the word, an adventurer. His voyage was undertaken with a view solely to his own advantage, the gratification of an incredible avarice. In the lust of gold he committed deeds of cruelty, treachery and oppression for which no fitting names are found in the vocabulary of any modern tongue. To the harmless and hospitable peoples among whom he came he was a terror and a curse. He tortured them, he murdered them, he sent them over the sea as slaves. So monstrous were his crimes, so conscienceless his ambition, so insatiable his greed, so black his treachery to his sovereign, that in his mere imprisonment and disgrace we have a notable instance of "the miscarriage of justice." In the black abysm of this man's character we may pile falsehood upon falsehood, but we shall never build the monument high enough to top the shadow of his shame. Upon the culm and crown of that reverend pile every angel will still look down and weep.

We are told that Columbus was no worse than the men of his race and generation—that his vices were "those of his time." No vices are peculiar to any time; this world has been vicious from the dawn of history, and every race has reeked with sin. To say of a man that he is like his contemporaries is to say that he is a scoundrel without excuse. The virtues are accessible to all. Athens was vicious, yet Socrates was virtuous. Rome was corrupt, but Marcus Aurelius was not corrupt. To offset Nero the gods gave Seneca. When literary France groveled at the feet of the third Napoleon Hugo stood erect.

It will be a dark day for the world when infractions of the moral law by A and B are accepted as justification of the sins of C. But even in the days of Columbus men were not all pirates; God inspired enough of them to be merchants to serve as prey for the others; and while turning his honest penny by plundering them, the great Christopher was worsted by a Venetian trading galley and had to pickle his pelt in a six-mile swim to the Portuguese coast, a wiser and a wetter thief. If he had had the hard luck to drown we might none of us have been Americans, but the gods would have missed the revolting spectacle of an entire people prostrate before the blood-beslubbered image of a moral idiot, performing solemn rites of adoration with a litany of lies.

In comparison with the crimes of Columbus his follies cut a sorry figure. Yet the foolhardy enterprise to whose failure he owes his fame is entitled to distinction. With sense enough to understand the earth's spheroid form (he thought it pear-shaped) but without knowledge of its size, he believed that he could reach India by sailing westward and died in the delusion that he had done so—a trifling miscalculation—a matter of eight or ten thousands of miles. If this continent had not happened to lie right across his way he and his merry men would all have gone fishing, with themselves for bait and the devil a hook among them. Firmness is persistence in the right; obstinacy is persistence in the wrong. With the light that he had, Columbus was so wildly, dismally and fantastically wrong that his refusal to turn back was nothing less than pig-headed unreason, and his crews would have been abundantly justified in deposing him. The wisdom of an act is not to be determined by the outcome, but by the performer's reasonable expectation of success. And after all, the expedition failed lamentably. It accomplished no part of its purpose, but by a happy chance it accomplished something better—for us. As to the red Indians, such of them as have been good enough to assist in apotheosis of the man whom their ancestors had the deep misfortune to discover may justly boast themselves the most magnanimous of mammals.

And when all is conceded there remains the affronting falsehood that Columbus discovered America. Surely in all these drunken orgies of beatification—in all this carnival of lies there should be found some small place for Leif Ericsson and his wholesome Northmen, who discovered, colonized and abandoned this continent five hundred years before, and of whom we are forbidden to think as corsairs and slave-catchers. The eulogist is always a calumniator. The crown that he sets upon the unworthy head he first tears from the head that is worthy. So the honest fame of Leif Ericsson is cast as rubbish to the void, and the Genoese pirate is pedestaled in his place.

But falsehood and ingratitude are sins against Nature, and Nature is not to be trifled with. Already we feel, or ought to feel, the smart of her lash. Our follies are finding us out. Our Columbian Exhibition has for its chief exhibit our national stupidity, and displays our shame. Our Congress "improves the occasion" to make a disgraceful surrender to the Chadbands and Stigginses of churches by a bitter observance of the Sabbath. Managers of the show steal the first one thousand dollars that come into their hands by bestowing them upon a schoolgirl related to one of themselves, for a "Commemoration Ode" as long as the language and as foolish as its grammar—the ragged, tagless and bobtailed yellow dog of commemoration odes. And *this* while Whittier lived to suffer the insult, and Holmes to resent it. What further exhibits of our national stupidity and lack of moral sense space has been engaged for in the world's contempt one can only conjecture. In the meantime state appropriations are being looted, art is in process of caricature, literature is debauched, and we have a Columbian Bureau of Investigation and Suppression with a daily mail as voluminous as that of a commercial city. If at the finish of this revealing revelry self-respecting Americans shall not have lost through excessive use the power to blush, and all Europe the ability to laugh, another Darwin should write another book on the expression of the emotions in men and animals.

That nothing might be lacking to the absurdity of the scheme, the falsehood marking all the methods of its execution, we must needs avail ourselves of an alteration in the calendar and have two anniversary celebrations of one event. And in culmination of this comedy of falsehood, the later date must formally open, with dedicatory rites, an exhibition which will not be open for six months. One falsehood begets another and another in the line of succession, until the father of them all shall have colonized his whole progeny upon the congenial soil of this new Dark Continent.

Why should not the four-hundredth anniversary of the rediscovery of America have been made memorable by fitly celebrating it with a becoming sense of the stupendous importance of the event, without thrusting into the forefront of the rites the dismal personality of the very small man who made the find? Could not the most prosperous and vain people of the earth see anything to celebrate in the four centuries between San Salvador and Chicago but it must sophisticate history by picking that offensive creature out of his shame to make him a central, dominating figure of the festival? Thank Heaven, there is one thing that all the genius of the anthropolaters can not do. Quarrel as we may about the relative claims to authenticity of portraits painted from description, we can not perpetuate the rogue's visible appearance "in his habit as he lived." Audible to the ear of the understanding fall with unceasing iteration from the lips of his every statue in every land the words, "I am a lie!"

1892.

THE CLOTHING OF GHOSTS

Belief in ghosts and apparitions is general, almost universal; possibly it is shared by the ghosts themselves. We are told that this wide distribution of the faith and its persistence through the ages are powerful evidences of its truth. As to that, I do not remember to have heard the basis of the argument frankly stated; it can be nothing else than that whatever is generally and long believed is true, for of course there can be nothing in the particular belief under consideration making it peculiarly demonstrable by counting noses. The world has more Buddhists than Christians. Is Buddhism therefore the truer religion? Before the day of Galileo there was a general though not quite universal conviction that the earth was a motionless body, the sun passing around it daily. That was a matter in which "the united testimony of mankind" ought to have counted for more than it should in the matter of ghosts, for all can observe the earth and sun, but not many profess to see ghosts, and no one holds that the circumstances in which they are seen are favorable to calm and critical observation. Ghosts are notoriously addicted to the habit of evasion; Heine says that it is because they are afraid of us. "The united testimony of mankind" has a notable knack at establishing only one thing—the incredibility of the witnesses.

If the ghosts care to prove their existence as objective phenomena they are unfortunate in always discovering themselves to inaccurate observers, to say nothing of the bad luck of frightening them into fits. That the seers of ghosts are inaccurate observers, and therefore incredible witnesses, is clear from their own stories. Who ever heard of a naked ghost? The apparition is always said to present himself (as he certainly should) properly clothed, either "in his habit as he lived" or in the apparel of the grave. Herein the witness must be at fault: whatever power of apparition after dissolution may inhere in mortal flesh and blood, we can hardly be expected to believe that cotton, silk, wool and linen have the same mysterious gift. If textile fabrics had that property they would sometimes manifest it independently, one would think—would "materialize" visibly without a ghost inside, a greatly simpler apparition than "the grin without the cat."

Ask any proponent of ghosts if he think that the products of the loom can "revisit the glimpses of the moon" after they have duly decayed, or, while still with us, can show themselves in a place where they are not. If he have no suspicion, poor man, of the trap set for him, he will pronounce the thing impossible and absurd, thereby condemning himself out of his own mouth; for assuredly such powers in these material things are necessary to the garmenting of spooks.

Now, by the law *falsus in uno falsus in omnibus* we are compelled to reject all the ghost stories that have ever been seriously told. If the observer (let him be credited with the best intentions) has observed so badly as to think he saw what he did not see, and could not have seen, in one particular, to what credence is he entitled with regard to another? His error in the matter of the "long white robe" or other garment where no long white robe or other garment could be puts him out of court altogether. Resurrection of woolen, linen, silk, fur, lace, feathers, hooks and eyes, buttons, hat-pins and the like—well, really, that is going far.

No, we draw the line at clothing. The materialized spook appealing to our senses for recognition of his ghostly character must authenticate himself otherwise than by familiar and remembered habiliments. He must be credentialed by nudity —and that regardless of temperature or who may happen to be present. Nay, it is to be feared that he must eschew his hair, as well as his habiliments, and "swim into our ken" utterly bald; for the scientists tell us with becoming solemnity that hair is a purely vegetable growth and no essential part of us. If he deem these to be hard conditions he is at liberty to remain on his reservation and try to endow us with a terrifying sense of himself by other means.

In brief, the conditions under which the ghost must appear in order to command the faith of an enlightened world are so onerous that he may prefer to remain away—to the unspeakable impoverishment of letters and art.

1902.

ACTORS AND ACTING

I

Was Sir Henry Irving a great actor? Possibly; there is abundant testimony, little evidence. The testimony of Englishmen is to be received with caution, for Irving was an Englishman; that of Americans with greater caution, for the same reason. The narrowest provincialism in the world is that of great cities, and London is the greatest city. What London says all England repeats; and America affirms it on oath. It is understood, as a matter of course, that in the judgment of England the best English actor, writer or artist is the best in the world. If one has conquered his way to the foremost place in the approval of a small London clique, not, in the case of an actor, exceeding a half-dozen men promoted to power by a process of selection with which ability has had nothing to do, one has conquered half the world. It would be easy to name the half-dozen who made Henry Irving's fame and set it sailing o'er the seas with bellying canvas and flag apeak. On this side no one ever demanded the ship's papers. This is Echoland, home of the ditto-maniac. We are freemen, but not bigoted ones.

For aught I know Irving may have been as good an actor as his countrymen who saw him thought him. Nay, he may have been half as good as my countrymen who did not see him think him. I myself saw him play only two or three times. He was not then a good actor, but that was a long time before his death; judgment from the fading memory of a performance decades ago would hardly do. Wherein, then, lies excuse of this present infervency—this cry *qui vive* at the outpost of the camp? Herein. Not only were Irving's credentials defective; there is a strong presumption that the defect was irreparable—that they "certificate a sham." This defect was racial. The English are, if not an unemotional, an undermonstrative people. When sad the Englishman does not weep, when pleased he does not laugh. Anger him and he will neither stamp nor tear his hair; startle him and he jumps not an inch. His conversation is destitute of vivacity and unaided by gesticulation. His face does not light up when he deems it his duty to smile. His transports of affection are moderated to the seemly ceremony of shaking hands; though he is said sometimes to kiss his grandmother if she is past seventy and will let him. Removed from his brumous environment, the English human being becomes in time accessible to light and heat—penetrable by the truth that all manifestation of emotion and sentiment is not necessarily vulgar; but in the tight little isle Stolidity holds her immemorial sway without other change in the administrative function than occasional substitution of the stare of deprecation for the stare of complacency.

To suppose that great actors can come of a race like that is to trifle with the laws of nature. Acting is preëminently the art of expression—expression of the sentiments and emotions by speech, look, gesture, movement—in every way that one person can address the eye and ear of another. It requires the acutest and alertest sensibilities, faculties all responsive to subtle stirs of feeling. Are these English characteristics? Clearly not; they are those of the peoples that (in England) are despised as "volatile," "garrulous," "excitable"—the French and Italians, for examples, who have produced the only really good actors of modern times. Our own actors are better than the English, but not good; one sees better acting about a dining-table in Paris than has ever been seen on the stage of London or New York—excepting when it is held by players in whose veins is the fire of Southern suns, whose nerves dance to the rhythmic beat of Mediterranean ripples and

> keep, with Capri's sunny fountains,
> Perpetual holiday.

One pale globule of our cold Teutonic blood queers the whole performance. For German, English and American actors society should provide "homes," with light employment, good plain food and, when they keep their mouths shut and their limbs quiet, thunders of artificial applause.

II

Few respectable shams are to me more distasteful than the affectation of delight in the performance of an actor who speaks his lines in a tongue unknown to the audience, as did sometimes the late Signor Rossi in the rôle of "Otello." It is of the essence and validity of acting that it address the understanding through the ear as well as the eye. The tones of an actor's voice, however pleasing, do not address the understanding at all without intelligible words; they are no more than the notes of a violin—the pleasure they give is purely sensual, and the speaker might as well articulate no words at all. A play, or a part in a play, performed in unfamiliar speech is hardly better than a pantomime, and those who profess to find in it an intellectual gratification—well, they may be very estimable persons, for aught I know.

It is not enough, in order to enjoy "Othello" or "Hamlet," that the audience have a general familiarity with the part; their knowledge of it must be minute and precise. They must know of what particular sentiment a facial expression is the visible exponent; of what particular word a gesture is the accompaniment. Else how can they know that the look is natural, the motion impressive? If one had memorized the part *verbatim,* and the meaning of every word, the accidental omission of a sentence would break the chain, and all that the eye should afterward report of the passage would be meaningless. How shall you know that the actor "suits the action to the word" if you know not the word? To a mind ignorant of Italian the "Otello" of Signor Rossi may have been a noble exercise in guessing; as acting it can have had no value.

III

We are all familiar with the hoary old dictum that the public has no concern with the private lives of the show folk. I must ask leave to differ. I must insist that the public has a most serious interest in the chastity of girls and the fidelity of wives. It is not good for the public that its women be taught by conspicuous example that to her who possesses a single talent, or any number of talents, a life of shame is no bar to public adulation. Every young and inexperienced woman believes herself to have some commanding quality which properly fostered will bring her fame. If she knows that she can do nothing else she thinks that she can write poetry. Is not the father mad who shows his ambitious daughter how little men really care for virtue—how tolerant they are of vice if it be gilded with genius? Worse and most shameful of all, women who clutch away their skirts from contact with some poor devil of a girl who having soiled herself is unable to sing herself out of the mire, will take their pure young girls to see the world worshiping at the feet of a wanton and her paramour because, forsooth, both are gifted and one is beautiful. Let these tender younglings lay well to heart the lesson in charity. Let them not forget that in their parents' judgment an uncommon physical formation, joined with an exceptional talent, excuses an immoral life.

Talent? Beauty alone is all-sufficient. Was not the whole eastern half of this continent, at one time, overhung with clouds of incense burned at the shrine of Beauty unadorned with virtue? Did not the western half give it hospitable welcome and set the wreath upon a brow still reeking of a foreign lecher's royal kisses and the later salutes of an impossible gambler? She was not even an actress—she could play nothing but the devil. The foundation of her fame and fortune was scandal—scandal lacking even the excuse of love. She had the sagacity to boast of a distinction that she enjoyed in common with a hundred less thrifty dames. She knew the shortest cut to the American heart and pocket. She knew that American fathers, husbands, brothers, sons and lovers would be so base as to come and bring her gold, and that American mothers, wives, sisters, daughters and sweethearts would be bad enough to accompany them, to gaze without a blush at the posings of a simpleton recommended by a prince. She gathered her sheaves and went away. She came back to the re-ripening harvest, hoping that God would postpone the destruction of a corrupt land until she could get out of it.

Heaven forbid that I should set myself up as a censor of any offenders save those who have the hardihood to continue infamous; I only beg to point out that when Christ shielded the woman taken in adultery he did not tell her that if she were a good singer she might go her way and sin more. That is how I answer the ever-ready sneer about "casting the first stone." That is how I cast it. If the fallen woman, finding herself possessed of a single talent, had gone into business as a show without reforming her private morals Christ would not have been found standing all night in line to buy tickets for himself and the Blessed Virgin.

I am for preserving the ancient, primitive distinction between right and wrong. The virtues of Socrates, the wisdom of Aristotle, the examples of Marcus Aurelius and Jesus Christ are good enough to engage my admiration and rebuke my life. From my fog-scourged and plague-smitten morass I lift reverent eyes to the shining summits of eternal truth, where they stand; I strain my senses to catch the law that they deliver. In every age and clime vice and folly have shared the throne of a double dominance, dictating customs and fashions. At no time has the devil been idle, but his freshest work few eyes are gifted with the faculty to discover. We trace him where the centuries have hardened his tracks into history, but round about us his noiseless footfalls awaken no sense of his near activity.

The subject is too serious to be humorously discussed. This glorification of the world's higher harlotage is one of the great continental facts that no ingenuity, no sophistry, no sublimity of lying can circumnavigate. It marks a civilization that is ripe and rotten. It characterizes an age that has lost the landmarks of right reason. These actors and actresses of untidy lives—they reek audibly. We should not speak of going to see them; "I am going to smell Miss Molocha Montflummery in 'Juliet'"—that would adequately describe the moral situation. Brains and hearts these persons have none; they are destitute of manners, modesty and sense. The sight of their painted faces, the memory of their horrible slang, their simian cleverness, their vulgar *"aliases,"* their dissolute lives, half emotion and half wine—these are a sickness to any cleanly soul.

Moreover, I advance the belief that any woman who publicly, for gain or glory, charity or caprice, makes public exhibition of any talent or grace that she may happen to have, maculates the chastity of her womanhood, and is thenceforth unworthy of a manly love. No man of sensibility but feels a twinge on reading his wife's, or his sister's, or his daughter's name in print; none but trembles to hear it upon the lips of strangers. You might easily prove the absurdity of this feeling; but she is the wisest, and cleanest, and sweetest, and best beloved who is not at the pains to disregard it. Gentlemen, charge your glasses—here's a health to the woman that is not a show.

1893.

DID WE EAT ONE ANOTHER?

There is no doubt of it. The unwelcome truth has been long suppressed by interested parties who find their account in playing sycophant to that self-satisfied tyrant Modern Man; but to the impartial philosopher it is as plain as the nose upon the elephant's face that our ancestors ate one another. The custom of the Fiji Islanders, which is their only stock-in-trade, their only claim to notoriety, is a relic of barbarism; but it is a relic of our barbarism.

Man is naturally a carnivorous animal. That none but green-grocers will dispute. That he was formerly less vegetarian in his diet than at present, is clear from the fact that market gardening increases in the ratio of civilization. So we may safely assume that at some remote period Man subsisted on an exclusively flesh diet. Our uniform vanity has given us the human mind as the acme of intelligence, the human face and figure as the standard of beauty. Of course we cannot deny to human fat and lean an equal superiority over beef, mutton and pork. It is plain that our meat-eating ancestors would think in this way, and being unrestrained by the mawkish sentiment attendant on high civilization, would act habitually on the obvious suggestion. *A priori,* therefore, it is clear that we ate ourselves.

Philology is about the only thread that connects us with the prehistoric past. By picking up and piecing together the scattered remnants of language, we form a patchwork of wondrous design and significance. Consider the derivation of the word "sarcophagus," and see if it be not suggestive of potted meats. Observe the significance of the phrase "sweet sixteen." What a world of meaning lurks in the expression "she is as sweet as a peach," and how suggestive of luncheon are the words "tender youth." A kiss is but a modified bite, and a fond mother, when she says her babe is "almost good enough to eat," merely shows that she is herself only a trifle too good to eat it.

These evidences might be multiplied *ad infinitum;* but if enough has been said to induce one human being to revert to the diet of his forefathers the object of this essay is accomplished.

1868.

CHRISTMAS AND THE NEW YEAR

In our manner of observing Christmas there is much, no doubt, that is absurd. Christmas is to some extent a day of meaningless ceremonies, false sentiment and hollow compliments endlessly iterated and misapplied. The observances "appropriate to the day" had, many of them, their origin in an age with which our own has little in common and in countries whose social and religious characteristics were unlike those obtaining here. As in so many other matters, America has in this been content to take her heritage without inquiry and without alteration, sacredly preserving much that once had a meaning now lost, much that is now an anachronism, a mere "survival." Even to the Christmas vocabulary we have added little. St. Nicholas himself, the patron saint of deceived children, still masquerades under the Spanish feminine title of "Santa" and the German nickname of "Claus." The back of our American coal grate is still idealized as a "yule log," and the English "holly" is supposed in most cases fitly to be shadowed forth by a cedar bough, while a comparatively innocuous but equally inedible indigenous comestible figures as the fatal English "plum pudding." Nearly all our Christmas literature is, *longo intervallo,* European in spirit and Dickensish in form. In short, we have Christmas merely because we were in the line of succession. We have taken it as it was transmitted, and we try to make the worst of it.

The approach of the season is apparent in the manner of the friend or relative whose orbs furtively explore your own, seeking a sign of what you are going to give him; in the irrepressible solicitations of babes and cloutlings; in wild cascades of such literature as *Greenleaf on Evidence, for Boys* ("Boot-Leg" series), *The Little Girls' Illustrated Differential Calculus* and *Aunt Hetty's Rabelais,* in words of one syllable. Most clearly is the advent of the blessed anniversary manifest in maddening iteration of the greeting wherein, with a precision that never by any chance mistakes its adjective, you are wished a "merry" Christmas by the same person who a week later will be making ninety-nine "happies" out of a possible hundred in New Year greetings similarly insincere and similarly insufferable. It is unknown to me why a Christmas should be always merry but never happy, and why the happiness appropriate to the New Year should not be expressed in merriment. These be mysteries in whose penetration abundance of human stupidity might be disclosed. By the time that one has been wished a "merry Christmas" or a "happy New Year" some scores of times in the course of a morning walk, by persons who he knows care nothing about either his merriment or his happiness, he is disposed, if he is a person of right feeling, to take a pessimist view of the "compliments of the season" and of the season of compliments. He cherishes, according to disposition, a bitter animosity or a tolerant contempt toward his race. He relinquishes for another year his hope of meeting some day a brilliant genius or inspired idiot who will have the intrepidity to vary the adjective and wish him a "happy Christmas" or a "merry New Year"; or with an even more captivating originality, keep his mouth shut.

As to the sum of sincerity and genuine good will that utters itself in making and accepting gifts (the other distinctive feature of holiday time) statistics, unhappily, are wanting and estimates untrustworthy. It may reasonably be assumed that the custom, though largely a survival—gifts having originally been given in a propitiatory way by the weak to the powerful—is something more; the present of a goggle-eyed doll from a man six feet high to a baby twenty-nine inches long not being lucidly explainable by assumption of an interested motive.

To the children the day is delightful and instructive. It enables them to see their elders in all the various stages of interesting idiocy, and teaches them by means of the Santa Claus deception that exceedingly hard liars may be good mothers and fathers and miscellaneous relatives—thus habituating the infant mind to charitable judgment and establishing an elastic standard of truth that will be useful in their later life.

The annual recurrence of the "carnival of crime" at Christmas has been variously accounted for by different authorities. By some it is supposed to be a providential dispensation intended to heighten the holiday joys of those who are fortunate enough to escape with their lives. Others attribute it to the lax morality consequent upon the demand for presents, and still others to the remorse inspired by consciousness of ruinous purchases. It is affirmed by some that persons deliberately and with malice aforethought put themselves in the way of being killed, in order to avert the tiresome iteration of Christmas greetings. If this is correct, the annual Christmas "holocaust" is not an evil demanding abatement, but a blessing to be received in a spirit of devout and pious gratitude.

When the earth in its eternal circumgression arrives at the point where it was at the same time the year before, the sentimentalist whom Christmas has not exhausted of his essence squeezes out his pitiful dreg of emotion to baptize the New Year withal. He dusts and polishes his aspirations, and reërects his resolve, extracting these well-worn properties from the cobwebby corners of his moral lumber-room, whither they were relegated three hundred and sixty-four days before. He "swears off." In short, he sets the centuries at defiance, breaks the sequence of cause and effect, repeals the laws of nature and makes himself a new disposition from a bit of nothing left over at the creation of the universe. He can not add an inch to his stature, but thinks he can add a virtue to his character. He can not shed his nails, but believes he can renounce his vices. Unable to eradicate a freckle from his skin, he is confident he can decree a habit out of his conduct. An improvident friend of mine writes upon his mirror with a bit of soap the cabalistic word, AFAHMASP. This is the *fiat lux* to create the shining virtue of thrift, for it means, A Fool And His Money Are Soon Parted. What need have we of morality's countless ministries; the complicated machinery of the church; recurrent suasions of precept and unceasing counsel of example; pursuing din of homily; still, small voice of solicitude and inaudible argument of surroundings—if one may make of himself what he will with a mirror and a bit of soap? But (it may be urged) if one can not reform himself, how can he reform others? Dear reader, let us have a frank understanding. He can not.

The practice of inflating the midnight steam-shrieker and belaboring the nocturnal ding-dong to frighten the encroaching New Year is obviously ineffectual, and might profitably be discontinued. It is no whit more sensible and dignified than the custom of savages who beat their sounding dogs to scare away an eclipse. If one elect to live with barbarians, one must endure the barbarous noises of their barbarous superstitions, but the disagreeable simpleton who sits up till midnight to ring a bell or fire a gun because the earth has arrived at a given point in its orbit should nevertheless be deprecated as an enemy to his race. He is a sore trial to the feelings, an affliction almost too sharp for endurance. If he and his sentimental abettors might be melted and cast into a great bell, every right-minded man would derive an innocent delight from pounding it, not only on January first but all the year long.

ON PUTTING ONE'S HEAD INTO ONE'S BELLY

Mr. Henry Holt, a publisher, has uttered his mind at no inconsiderable length in deprecation of what he calls "the commercialization of literature." That literature, in this country and England at least, has somewhat fallen from its high estate and is regarded even by many of its purveyors as a mere trade is unfortunately true, as we see in the genesis and development of the "literary syndicates"; in the unholy alliance between the book reviewer and the head of the advertising department; in the systematic "booming" of certain books and authors by methods, both supertabular and submanual, not materially different from those used for the promotion of a patent medicine; in the reverent attitude of editors and publishers toward authors of "best sellers," and in more things than can be here set down. In the last century when, surely by no fortuitous happening, American literature was made by such men as Irving, Cooper, Bryant, Poe, Emerson, Whittier, Hawthorne, Longfellow, Holmes and Lowell, these purely commercial phenomena were in less conspicuous evidence and some of them were altogether indiscernible.

That the period of literature's commercialization should be that of its decay is obviously more than a coincidence. Mr. Holt observes both, and is sad, but *that* is a coincidence pure and simple: his melancholy is due to something else. The "commercialization" is confessedly compelling him to do a good deal more advertising than he likes to pay for; for commerce spells competition. The authors of to-day and their agents have acquired the disagreeable habit of taking their wares to the highest bidder—the publisher who will give the highest royalties and the broadest publicity. The immemorial relation whereby the publisher was said to drink wine out of the author's skull has been rudely disturbed by the latter demanding some of the wine for himself and refusing to supply the skull—an irritating infraction of a good understanding sanctified by centuries of faithful observance. It is only natural that Mr. Holt, being a conservative man and a protagonist of established order, should experience some of the emotions appropriate to the defenders in a servile insurrection.

With a candor that is most becoming, Mr. Holt expressly bewails the passing of the old régime—the departed days when authors "had other resources" than authorship. This is the second time that it has been my melancholy privilege to hear the head of a prosperous American publishing house make this moan. Another one, a few years ago, in addressing a company of authors, solemnly advised them to have some means of support additional to writing. I was not then, and am not now, assured that publishers find it necessary to have any means of support additional to publishing.

THE AMERICAN CHAIR

A London philosopher was once pleased to remark that the American habit of sitting on the middle of the back with the feet elevated might in time profoundly alter the American physical structure, producing a race having its type in the Bactrian camel. If "our cousins across the water" understood this matter they would not adopt the flippant tone toward us that they now do, but in place of ridicule would bestow compassion. Before endeavoring to clear away the misconceptions surrounding the subject, so as to let in upon ourselves the holy light of British sympathy I must explain that the practice of sitting in the manner which the British philosopher somewhat inaccurately describes is confined mostly to the males of our race; the American woman will not, I trust, partake of the structural modification foreseen by the scientific eye, but remain, as now, simply and sweetly dromedarian. True, Nature may punish her for being found in bad company, but at the first stroke of the lash she will doubtless forsake us and seek sanctuary in the companionship of that bolt-upright vertebrate, the English nobleman.

The national peculiarity which, one is sorry to observe, provokes nothing but levity in the British mind—and British levity is no light affliction—is not our fault but our misfortune. Like every other people, we Americans are the slaves of those who serve us. Not one of us in a thousand (so busy are we in "subduing the wilderness" and guarding our homes against the Redskins) has leisure to plan and order his surroundings; and to the few whom Fortune has favored with leisure she has denied the means. We take everything ready-made—our houses, grounds, carriages, furniture and all. In some of these things Providence has by special interposition introduced new designs and revived old ones, but in most of them there is neither change nor the shadow of turning. They are to-day what they were a century ago, and a century hence will be what they are to-day. The chairmaker, for example, is the obscure intelligence and indirigible energy that his grandfather was before him: the American chair maintains through the ages its bad eminence as an instrument of torture. Time can not wither nor custom stale its infinite malevolence. The type of the species is the familiar hardpan chair of the kitchen; in the dining-room this has been deplaced by the "splint-bottom," and in the parlor by an armed and upholstered abomination which tempts us to session only to turn to ashes, as it were, upon our bodies. They are essentially the same old chair—worthy descendants of the original Adam of Chairs, created from a block in the image of its maker's head. The American chair is never made to measure; it is supposed to fit anybody and be universally applicable.

It is to the American chair that we must look for the genesis and rationale of the American practice of shelving the American feet on the most convenient dizzy eminence. We naturally desire as little contact with the chair as possible, so we touch it with the acutest angle that we are able to achieve. The feet must rest somewhere, and a place must be found for them. It is admitted that the mantel, the sideboard, the window-sill, the *escritoire* and the dining table (at least during meals) are not good places; but *que voulez vous?*—the chairmakers have not chosen to invent anything to mitigate the bitterness of the situation as by their genius for evil they have made it.

I humbly submit that in all this there is nothing deserving of ridicule. It is a situation with a pathos of its own, which ought to appeal strongly to a people suffering so many of the ills of conservitude, as do the English. It is all very well (to use their own pet locution) to ask why we do not abolish the American chair, but really the question ought not to come from a nation that endures *Mr. Punch,* pities the House of Lords and embraces that of Hanover. The

American chair was probably divinely designed and sent upon us for the chastening of our national spirit, and we accept it with the same reverent submission that distinguishes our English critic in bowing his neck to the heavy yoke of his own humor.

DISINTRODUCTIONS

The devil is a citizen of every country, but only in our own are we in constant peril of an introduction to him. That is democracy. All men are equal; the devil is a man; therefore, the devil is equal. If that is not a good and sufficient syllogism I should be pleased to know what is the matter with it.

To write in riddles when one is not prophesying is too much trouble; what I am affirming is the horror of the characteristic American custom of promiscuous, unsought and unauthorized introductions.

You incautiously meet your friend Smith in the street; if you had been prudent you would have remained indoors. Your helplessness makes you desperate and you plunge into conversation with him, knowing entirely well the disaster that is in cold storage for you.

The expected occurs: another man comes along and is promptly halted by Smith and you are introduced! Now, you have not given to the Smith the right to enlarge your circle of acquaintance and select the addition himself; why did he do this thing? The person whom he has condemned you to shake hands with may be an admirable person, though there is a strong numerical presumption against it; but for all that the Smith knows he may be your bitterest enemy. The Smith has never thought of that. Or you may have evidence (independent of the fact of the introduction) that he is some kind of thief—there are one thousand and fifty kinds of thieves. But the Smith has never thought of that. In short, the Smith has never thought. In a Smithocracy all men, as aforesaid, being equal, all are equally agreeable to one another.

That is a logical extension of the Declaration of American

Independence. If it is erroneous the assumption that a man will be pleasing to me because he is pleasing to another is erroneous too, and to introduce me to one that I have not asked nor consented to know is an invasion of my rights—a denial and limitation of my liberty to a voice in my own affairs. It is like determining what kind of clothing I shall wear, what books I shall read, or what my dinner shall be.

In calling promiscuous introducing an American custom I am not unaware that it obtains in other countries than ours. The difference is that in those it is mostly confined to persons of no consequence and no pretensions to respectability; here it is so nearly universal that there is no escaping it. Democracies are naturally and necessarily gregarious. Even the French of to-day are becoming so, and the time is apparently not distant when they will lose that fine distinctive social sense that has made them the most punctilious, because the most considerate, of all nations excepting the Spanish and the Japanese. By those who have lived in Paris since I did I am told that the chance introduction is beginning to devastate the social situation, and men of sense who wish to know as few persons as possible can no longer depend on the discretion of their friends.

To say so is not the same thing as to say "Down with the republic!" The republic has its advantages. Among these is the liberty to say, "Down with the republic!"

It is to be wished that some great social force, say a billionaire, would set up a system of disintroductions. It should work somewhat like this:

Mr. White—Mr. Black, knowing the low esteem in which you hold each other, I have the honor to disintroduce you from Mr. Green.

Mr. Black (*bowing*)—Sir, I have long desired the advantage of your unacquaintance.

Mr. Green (*bowing*)—Charmed to unmeet you, sir. Our acquaintance (the work of a most inconsiderate and unworthy person) has distressed me beyond expression. We are greatly indebted to our good friend here for his tact in repairing the mischance.

Mr. White—Thank you. I'm sure you will become very good strangers.

This is only the ghost of a suggestion; of course the plan is capable of an infinite elaboration. Its capital defect is that the persons who are now so liberal with their unwelcome introductions, will be equally lavish with their disintroductions, and will estrange the best of friends with as little ceremony as they now observe in their more fiendish work.

1902.

THE LATE LAMENTED

How long one must be dead before his "relics"—including not only his remains proper, but the several appurtenances thereunto belonging—cease to be "sacred," is a question which has never been settled. London was once divided in opinion, or rather in feeling, as to the propriety of publicly exhibiting the body-linen worn by Charles I when that unhappy monarch had the uncommon experience of losing his head. Not only was this underwear shown, but also some of the royal hair which was cut away by the headsman. Many persons considered the exhibition distasteful and in a measure sacrilegious. But the entire body of the great Rameses has been dug out and is freely shown without provoking a protest.

Rameses was a mightier king than Charles, and a more famous. He was the veritable Pharaoh of sacred history whose daughter (who, I regret to say, was also his wife) found the infant Moses in the bulrushes. He could also point with pride to his record in profane history, and was, altogether, a most respectable person. Between the power, splendor and civilization of the Egypt of Rameses and the England of Charles there is no comparison: in the imperishable glory of the former the latter seems a nation of savage pigmies. Why, then, are the actual remains of the one monarch considered a fit and proper "exhibit" in a museum and the mere personal adornments of the other too sacred for desecration by the public eye? Probably political and ethnic considerations have something to do with it: perhaps in Cairo the sentiment would be the other way, though the stoical indifference of successive Egyptian Governments to mummy-mining by the thrifty European does not sustain that view.

Schliemann and many of his moling predecessors have dug up and removed the sleeping ancients from what these erroneously believed to be their last resting-places in Asia Minor and the other classic countries, without rebuke, and the funeral urn of an illustrious Roman can be innocently haled from its pigeon-hole in a *columbarium*. We open the burial mounds of our Indian predecessors and pack off their skulls with never a thought of wrong, and even the bones of our own early settlers when in course of removal to make way for a new city hall are treated with but scant courtesy. There seems to be no statute of limitations applicable to the sanctity of tombs; every case is judged on its merits, with a certain loose regard to local conditions and considerations of expediency.

It was an ancient belief that the shade of even the most worthy deceased could not enter Elysium so long as the body was unburied, but no provision was made for expulsion of those already in if their bodies were exhumed and used as "attractions" for museums. So we may reasonably hope that the companions of Agamemnon contemplate the existence of Schliemanns with philosophic indifference; and doubtless Rameses the Great, who, according to the religion of his country, had an immortality conditioned on the preservation of his mortal part, is as well content that it lie in a museum as in a pyramid.

MUSIC

Let him to whom, as to me, nature has denied "an ear for music," or circumstance an opportunity for its education, take heart and comfort: he has escaped a masterful temptation to commit nonsense in the first degree. Doubtless there are music makers and music lovers who can write and speak of the art with a decent regard to the demands of common sense, but doubtless they don't; their history is a record of ignored opportunities. As to the others—the chaps who push in between our hearing and our understanding—they possibly "play by note," but they write "by ear." They say whatever sounds well to themselves, and there they leave it. Theirs is the art of sound and they expound its principles with due observance of its results: in speaking of it they are satisfied to make a pleasant noise. The louder the noise of their exposition, the most glorious the art which it expounds. As members of mystic brotherhoods are bound by oath not to divulge the solemn secrets which they do not possess; as the married have a tacit undertaking to wreathe their chains with flowers, smile away their wounds, and exhibit as becoming ornaments the handles of the daggers rusting in their hearts; as priesthoods plate with gold their empty shrines; as the dead swear in stone and brass that they were virtuous and great—so the musical are in conspiracy to magnify and exalt their art. It is a pretty art: it is rich in elements of joy, purveying to the sense a refined and keen delight. But it is not what they say it is. It is not what the uninitiated believe it. What is?

I am led to these reflections—provoked were the better word—by reading one Krehbiel. "Wagner," Mr. Krehbiel explains, "strove to express artistic truths, not to tickle the ear, and therefore his work will stand, while Italian opera, which is founded on sensual enjoyment, must pass away." A more amusing *non sequitur* it would be difficult for the most accomplished logician to construct. Because the city is founded on a rock it will topple down! I think I could name several sorts of sensual enjoyment which give promise of enduring as long as the senses. Among them I should give a high place to whatever kind of music the sense of hearing most enjoys. If posterity is going to be such an infinite fool as to stop its ears to sounds which please them, I thank Heaven that I live in antiquity.

The enjoyment of music is a purely sensual enjoyment. It "tickles the ear," and it does nothing else. The ear being skilfully tickled after the fashion which the composer and the executant understand, emotion ensues; but not thought, save by association—by memory. Music does not touch the springs of the intellect. It never generated a process of reasoning, nor expressed a truth, "artistic" or other, which could be formulated in a definitive proposition. It has no intellectual character whatever. I have heard this disputed scores of times, but never by one who had himself much intellect. And, in truth, musicians, if I must say it, are not commonly distinguished above their fellows by mental capacity. The greater their gift, the less they know; and when you find a tremendously skilful and enthusiastic executant you will have as nearly sensual an animal as you care to catch.

To those having knowledge of the essential meaning of music, its original place among the influences that wrought their results upon primitive man, this will seem natural and sequent. Music was originally vocal; before men became wise enough and deft enough to make instruments they merely sang, as the birds do now, and certain animals—the latter pretty badly, it must be confessed. But why did the primitive man and woman sing? To commend themselves in the matter of love, as the birds do, and the beasts. Abundant vestiges of this practice survive among us. The young woman who bangs her piano and her hair has a single motive in the double habit. She is hardly conscious of it; she has inherited it along with the desire to brandish her eyes, and otherwise manslay. Consider, my tuneless youth, how slender is your chance in rivalry with the fellow who can sing. He will "knock you out" with a bar of music better than a Chinese highbinder could with a bar of iron. It did not occur to our good arboreal ancestor (him of the prehensile tail, aswing upon his branch) to address his wood-notes wild to a mixed audience for gate-money; he sought to charm a single pair of ears, and those more hairy than critical. Later, as the race went on humaning, there grew complexity of sentiment and varying emotional needs, for the gratification whereof song took on a matching complexity and variance. There were war songs, and death songs, and hunting songs, harvest songs and songs of adoration. Wood and metal were taught to perform acceptably.

> The shells of tortoises were made to sing,
> And, touched in tenderness, the captive string.

Did it ever occur to you, intelligent reader, that the

simplest musical instrument is a more astonishing invention than the talking phonograph? But the human love-tone is the soul and base of the system; and should men and women henceforth be born happily married the entire musical edifice would fade and vanish like a palace of clouds.

Selections from

THE MARCH HARE

"TO ELEVATE THE STAGE"

The existence of a theatrical company, composed entirely of Cambridge and Harvard *alumni* who have been in jail, strikes the imagination with a peculiar force. In the theatrical world the ideal condition conceived by certain social philosophers is being rapidly realized and reduced to practice. "It does not matter," say these superior persons, "what one does; it is only important what one is." The theater folk have long been taking that view of things, as is amply attested by the histrionic careers (for examples) of Mrs. Lily Langtry and Mr. John L. Sullivan. Managers—and, we may add, the public—do not consider it of the least importance what Mrs. Langtry *does* on the stage, nor how she does it, so long as she *is* a former favorite of a Prince and a tolerably fair counterpart of a Jersey cow. And who cares what Mr. Sullivan's pronunciation of the word "mother" may be, or what degree of sobriety he may strive to simulate?—in seeing his performance we derive all our delight from the consciousness of the great and godlike thing that he has the goodness to *be*.

It is needless to recall other instances; every playgoer's memory is richly stored with them; but this troupe of convicted collegians is the frankest application of the principle to which we have yet been treated. At the same time, it opens up "vistas" of possibilities extending far-and-away beyond what was but yesterday the longest reach of conjecture. Why should we stop with a troupe of educated felons? Let us recognize the principle to the full and apply it with logical heroism, unstayed by considerations of taste and sense. Let us have theater companies composed of reformed assassins who have been preachers. A company of deaf mutes whose grandfathers were hanged, would prove a magnetic "attraction" and play to good houses—that is to say, they would *be* to good houses. In a troupe of senators with warts on their noses the pleasure-shoving public would find an infinite gratification and delight. It might lack the allurement of feminine charm, most senators being rather old women, but for magnificent inaction it would bear the palm. Even better would be a company of distinguished corpses supporting some such star inactor, as the mummy of his late Majesty, Rameses II of Egypt. In them the do-nothing-be-something principle would have its highest, ripest and richest development. In the broad blaze of their histrionic glory Mrs. Langtry would pale her ineffectual fire and Mr. Sullivan hide his diminished head.

From the example of such a company streams of good would radiate in every direction, with countless ramifications. Not only would it accomplish the long desired "elevation of the stage" to such a plane that even the pulpit need not be ashamed to work with it in elicitation of the human snore, but it would spread the light over other arts and industries, causing "the dawn of a new era" generally. Even with the comparatively slow progress we are making now, it is not unreasonable to hope that eventually Man will cease his fussy activity altogether and do nothing whatever, each individual of the species becoming a veritable monument of philosophical inaction, rapt in the contemplation of his own abstract worth and perhaps taking root where he stands to survey it.

PECTOLITE

This is one of the younger group of minerals: it was discovered by a German scientist in 1828. For its age it is an exceptionally interesting stone—if it is a stone. Its most eminent and distinguishing peculiarity is described as the "property of parting with minute splinters from its surface upon being handled, these splinters or spicules piercing the hand, producing a pain similar to that experienced by contact with a nettle."

In the mineral kingdom pectolite ought to take high rank, near the very throne. In its power of annoying man it is a formidable competitor to several illustrious members of the vegetable kingdom, such as the nettle, the cactus, the poison ivy and the domestic briar. There are, indeed, several members of the animal kingdom which hardly excel it in the power of producing human misery. Considering its remarkable aptitude in that bad way its rarity is somewhat difficult to understand, and is perhaps more apparent than real. Professor Hanks says that previously to its discovery in California it had been found in only eight places. If upon investigation these should turn out to be Europe, Asia, Africa, North and South America, Australia and the two Polar continents, the unnatural discrepancy between its objectionable character and its narrow distribution would be explained away, and pectolite seen to be "in touch" with its sister malevolences, whose abundance is usually in the direct ratio of their noxiousness to man.

In his efforts to make this uncommon mineral known, advance its interests and bring it into closer relations with mankind, Professor Hanks is winning golden opinions from the manufacturer of arsenic, the promoter of the Canadian thistle, and the local agent of the imported rattlesnake. The various uses to which it can be put are obvious and numberless. As a missile in a riot—the impeller wearing a glove, but the other person having nothing to guard his face and eyes— its field of usefulness will be wide and fertile. Small fragments of it attractively displayed here and there about the city will give a rich return of agony when thoughtlessly picked up. For village sidewalks inimical to the thin shoe of the period it would be entirely superior to the knotty plank studded with projecting nail heads. With a view to these various "uses of adversity," it would be well for Professor Hanks to submit careful estimates of the cost of quarrying it and transporting it to places where it can be made to do the greatest harm to the greatest number. To assist and further the purposes of Nature, as manifested in the character of the several agencies and materials which she employs, is the greatest glory of science. A human being assailed by all the natural forces, seizing a stone to defend himself and getting a fistful of pectolitic spiculæ, is a spectacle in which one can get as near and clear a glimpse of the Great Mystery as in any; and science is now prepared to supply the stone.

A DUBIOUS VINDICATION

Hardly any class of persons enjoys complete immunity from injustice and calumny, even if "armed with the ballot"; but probably no class has so severely suffered from Slander's mordant tooth as our man-eating brethren of that indefinite region known as the "Cannibal Islands." Nations which do not eat themselves, and which, with even greater self-denial, refrain from banqueting on other nations, have for generations been subjected to a species of criticism that must be a sore trial to their patience. Every reprobate among us who has sense enough to push a pencil along the measured mile of a day's task in a newspaper office without telling the truth has experienced a sinful pleasure in representing anthropophagi as persons of imperfect refinement and ailing morals. They have been censured even, for murder; though surely it is kinder to take the life of a man whom you set apart for your dinner than to eat him struggling. It has been said of them that they are particularly partial to the flesh of missionaries.

It appears that this is not so. The Rev. Mr. Hopkins, of the Methodist Church, who returned to New York after a residence of fifteen years in the various islands of the South Pacific, assured his brethren that in all that period he could not recollect a single instance in which he was made to feel himself a comestible. He averred that his spiritual character was everywhere recognized, and so far as he knew he was never in peril of being put to the tooth.

His testimony, unluckily, has not the value that its obvious sincerity and truth merit. In point of physical structure he was conspicuously inedible; so much so, in truth, that an unsympathetic reporter coldly described him as "fibrous" and declared that in a country where appetizers are unknown and pepsin a medicine of the future, Mr. Hopkins could under no circumstances cut any figure as a viand. And this same writer meaningly inquired of the cartilaginous missionary the present address of one "Fatty Dawson."

Fully to understand the withering sarcasm of this inquiry it is necessary to know that the person whose whereabouts it was desired to ascertain was a co-worker of Mr. Hopkins in the same missionary field. His success in spreading the light was such as to attract the notice of the native king. In the last letter received from Mr. Dawson he explained that that potentate had just done him the honor to invite him to dinner.

Mr. Hopkins being a missionary, one naturally prefers his views to those of anyone who is still in the bonds of iniquity, and moreover, writes for the newspapers; nevertheless, I do not see that any harm would come of a plain statement of the facts in the case of the Rev. Mr. Dawson. He was not eaten by the dusky monarch—in the face of Mr. Hopkins' solemn assurance that cannibalism is a myth, it is impossible to believe that Mr. Dawson was himself the dinner to which he was invited. That he was eaten by Mr. Hopkins himself is a proposition so abysmally horrible that none but the hardiest and most impenitent calumniator would have the depravity to suggest it.

ANTEPENULTIMA

TAKING ONESELF OFF

A person who loses heart and hope through a personal bereavement is like a grain of sand on the seashore complaining that the tide has washed a neighboring grain out of sight. He is worse, for the bereaved grain can not help itself; it has to be a grain of sand and play the game of tide, win or lose; whereas he can quit—by watching his opportunity can "quit a winner." For sometimes we do beat "the man that keeps the table"—never in the long run, but infrequently and out of small stakes. But this is no time to "cash in" and go, for you can not take your little winning with you. The time to quit is when you have lost a big stake, your foolish hope of eventual success, your fortitude and your love of the game. If you stay in the game, which you are not compelled to do, take your losses in good temper and do not whine about them. They are hard to bear, but that is no reason why you should be.

But we are told with tiresome iteration that we are "put here" for some purpose (not disclosed) and have no right to retire until "summoned"—it may be by small-pox, it may be by the bludgeon of a blackguard, it may be by the kick of a cow; the "summoning" Power (said to be the same as the "putting" Power) has not a nice taste in the choice of messengers. That argument is not worth attention, for it is unsupported by either evidence or anything resembling evi-

dence. "Put here." Indeed! And by the keeper of the table!
We were put here by our parents—that is all that anybody
knows about it; and they had no authority and probably no
intention.

The notion that we have not the right to take our own
lives comes of our consciousness that we have not the courage. It is the plea of the coward—his excuse for continuing
to live when he has nothing to live for—or his provision
against such a time in the future. If he were not egotist as
well as coward he would need no excuse. To one who does
not regard himself as the center of creation and his sorrows
as throes of the universe, life, if not worth living, is also
not worth leaving. The ancient philosopher who was asked
why he did not die if, as he taught, life was no better than
death, replied: "Because death is no better than life." We
do not know that either proposition is true, but the matter
is not worth considering, for both states are supportable—life
despite its pleasures and death despite its repose.

It was Robert G. Ingersoll's opinion that there is rather
too little than too much suicide in the world—that people
are so cowardly as to live on long after endurance has ceased
to be a virtue. This view is but a return to the wisdom of
the ancients, in whose splendid civilization suicide had as
honorable place as any other courageous, reasonable and un-
selfish act. Antony, Brutus, Cato, Seneca—these were not of
the kind of men to do deeds of cowardice and folly. The
smug, self-righteous modern way of looking upon the act as
that of a craven or a lunatic is the creation of priests,
philistines and women. If courage is manifest in endurance
of profitless discomfort it is cowardice to warm oneself when
cold, to cure oneself when ill, to drive away mosquitoes, to
go in when it rains. The "pursuit of happiness," then, is not
an "unalienable right," for it implies avoidance of pain.

No principle is involved in this matter; suicide is justifi-
able or not, according to circumstances; each case is to be
considered on its merits, and he having the act under advisement is sole judge. To his decision, made with whatever
light he may chance to have, all honest minds will bow. The
appellant has no court to which to take his appeal. Nowhere
is a jurisdiction so comprehensive as to embrace the right of
condemning the wretched to life.

Suicide is always courageous. We call it courage in a soldier merely to face death—say to lead a forlorn hope—although he has a chance of life and a certainty of "glory." But the suicide does more than face death; he incurs it, and with a certainty, not of glory, but of reproach. If that is not courage we must reform our vocabulary.

True, there may be a higher courage in living than in dying. The courage of the suicide, like that of the pirate, is not incompatible with a selfish disregard of the rights of others—a cruel recreancy to duty and decency. I have been asked: "Do you not think it cowardly for a man to end his life, thereby leaving his family in want?" No, I do not; I think it selfish and cruel. Is not that enough to say of it? Must we distort words from their true meaning in order more effectually to damn the act and cover its author with a greater infamy? A word means something; despite the maunderings of the lexicographers, it does not mean whatever you want it to mean. "Cowardice" means a shrinking from danger, not a shirking of duty. The writer who allows himself as much liberty in the use of words as he is allowed by the dictionary-maker and by popular consent is a bad writer. He can make no impression on his reader, and would do better service at the ribbon-counter.

The ethics of suicide is not a simple matter; one can not lay down laws of universal application, but each case is to be judged, if judged at all, with a full knowledge of all the circumstances, including the mental and moral make-up of the person taking his own life—an impossible qualification for judgment. One's time, race and religion have much to do with it. Some peoples, like the ancient Romans and the modern Japanese, have considered suicide in certain circumstances honorable and obligatory; among ourselves it is held in disfavor. A man of sense will not give much attention to considerations of this kind, excepting in so far as they affect others, but in judging weak offenders they are to be taken into the account. Speaking generally, I should say that in our time and country the persons here noted (and some others) are justified in removing themselves, and that in some of them it is a duty:

One afflicted with a painful or loathsome and incurable disease.

One who is a heavy burden to his friends, with no prospect of their relief.

One threatened with permanent insanity.

One irreclaimably addicted to drunkenness or some similarly destructive or offensive habit.

One without friends, property, employment or hope.

One who has disgraced himself.

Why do we honor the valiant soldier, sailor, fireman? For obedience to duty? Not at all; that alone—without the peril —seldom elicits remark, never evokes enthusiasm. It is because he faced without flinching the risk of that supreme disaster, or what we feel to be such—death. But look you: the soldier braves the danger of death; the suicide braves death itself! The leader of the forlorn hope may not be struck. The sailor who voluntarily goes down with his ship may be picked up or cast ashore. It is not certain that the wall will topple until the fireman shall have descended with his precious burden. But the suicide—his is the foeman that has never missed a mark, his the sea that gives nothing back; the wall that he mounts bears no man's weight. And his, at the end of it all, is the dishonored grave where the wild ass of public opinion

> Stamps o'er his head but can not break his sleep.

Selection from

THE SAMPLE COUNTER

OUR TALES OF SENTIMENT

FROM "ONE WOMAN"

Gladys climbed to the balustrade of the bridge and, adjusting her skirts, plunged into the gloomiest forebodings.

"Why," she said, "should the future look so dark to one possessing all that fortune can donate?"

She added a number of profound reflections on the vanity of life, ending with a brilliant epigram. It had scarcely died upon her lips when Armitage arrived upon the tapis and took in the situation at a glance. Striding hastily forward, he bowed gracefully and signified a desire to know the cause of her abstraction. She burst into tears and complied with his wish. Then she flung herself about his neck and accorded full expression to her grief, which he delicately professed not to observe; for this noble figure had been educated in the best schools of European gentility.

FROM "BUT A SINGLE THOUGHT"

Seeing her proceeding away from him, perhaps forever, Auvergne intercepted her with an expression of regret for his rudeness, coupled with a plea for pardon. For a breathless instant she stayed her progress as if uncertain as to the degree of his offense, then resumed her pace till she reached the river's brim. With an unconscious prayer she sprang swooning into the breakers and was with difficulty prevented from meeting a watery grave.

FROM "A BELLE OF CASTILE"

Josephina had progressed but a brief distance into the garden when some inner sense proclaimed that she was followed: the crunching of a gentleman's heel upon the gravel was indisputable. Partially terrified, she sought concealment in the shrubbery that bordered the path on the one side and the other. It passed by her there in the moonlight, that dreadful sound, yet no one visible! It went on and on, growing fainter and fainter, like herself, and was lost to hearing. Then she remembered the tradition of the Invisible Knight and her heart smote her for the absence of faith with which she had so often greeted it.

"I am fitly punished," she conceded, "for my sceptical attitude. Henceforth, so far as the constitution of my mind will permit, I will be more hospitable to the convictions of the simple."

How she adhered to this expiational resolution we shall behold.

FROM "THE QUEEN'S CHAPERON"

The duke stepped from his carriage to a neighboring hill and cast his eye athwart his ancestral domain. "All this," he mused, "I must renounce if I comply with the queen's royal suggestion to fly with her to Rome. Is she worth the privation? I must have time to consider a transaction of such great importance."

Hastily entering his carriage, he haughtily bade the coachman drive him to some expensive hotel, whence he dispatched a delicately perfumed note to her Majesty, saying that he should be detained a few days by affairs of state, but assuring her of his uncommon fidelity. Then he retired to his couch and thought it all over in Italian. The next day he arose and fled rapidly.

FROM "THE UPLIFTING OF LENNOX"

On hearing the terrible news Myra fell supine to earth without delay!

"Is it nothing?" inquired Lennox. "Is it only a temporary indisposition?—will it soon pass?"

But Myra replied only with a significant pallor which told all too plainly what the most accomplished linguist would vainly have striven to express.

How long she lay unconscious we know not, but promptly on becoming her previous self she let fall a multitude of tears.

Lennox yielded to the requirements of etiquette and stole away.

FROM "BERTHA OF BOOTHA"

As they strolled along the Riviera the setting sun was just touching the summit of the Alps and firing them with an electrical glow. Turning to her, he looked into her beautiful eyes and thus expressed himself:

"Dearest, I am about to make an important statement."

She almost instantly divined the character of the communication that he referred to, and it affected her with perturbation. It was so sudden. "If," she remarked, "you could postpone the statement above mentioned until a more suitable occasion I should regard your forbearance with satisfaction."

"Very well," he replied, with coldness, "I will wait until we are not alone."

"Thank you, ever so much," she blushed, and all was silence. Later in the season he explained to her the trend of his affections, and she signified the pleasure that she derived from his preference.

FROM "HERTHA OF HOOTHA"

The moon rose in the east without a sound and the ripples on the bosom of the main ran silently to the beach. Hertha and Henri, having similar sensibilities, were equally overcome by the solemnity of the scene, and neither inaugurated a conversation. Their love was too true for utterance by human tongue. Thus they paced for a considerable period, when suddenly the silence was cut asunder by a woman's scream!

"I know that voice," cried Henri, hastily divesting himself of as many of his upper garments as, under the circumstances, he deemed it proper to do; "it is Minetta committing suicide!"

He immediately plunged into the Atlantic, while Hertha stood rooted to the sand, endeavoring to regulate her emotions. In a few moments, which seemed an age, he emerged from the deep, bearing the deceased, whom he tenderly flung at her rival's feet.

Then the survivors knelt and prayed in both English and French.

FROM "ETHEL SHANKS"

Ethel hastened slowly along the path leading to the cliff above the lake. The full moon was rising in the east, for the hour was midnight, and her warm radiance bathed the landscape in a blue languor.

To Ethel the sky had never seemed so blue, nor the Polyanthes tuberosa in her corsage so white. She drank joy with her every breath, and she breathed quickly from her exertion in climbing the eminence on which she stood. Hearing footprints approaching, she turned, and the baron stood before her! "I was hasty," he explained. "I should not have disclosed my love with such abruption. Permit me to withdraw my inconsiderate declaration."

Ethel's heart sank within her! She could not refuse him the desired permission; that would not have been genteel: and Ethel was under all circumstances the lady. So she beat back the tears and said:

"Please, sir, dismiss it from attention."

The cry of her broken heart was unheard by that callous ear, unaccustomed to the sad, sweet chords evoked from the harp of a dead hope. The nobleman lit his pipe and, his cruel errand performed, returned to his ancestral mansion. For one or two moments Ethel stood on the brink of eternity. Precipitating herself from the extreme edge, she awaited death with composure; she had done her full duty and had no fear of the Hereafter. . . . At the base of the precipice she came into violent contact with a large granite boulder and was no more.

They found her body at the feet of the cliff, and the

baron was torn by conflicting emotions, for the head lay at some distance from the trunk, a truly melancholy spectacle.

"Can it be possible," he remarked, "that she is no more?"

Assured by the physician that such was the fact, he signified a high degree of regret and strode from the spot unattended; and to this day his fate is cloaked in the impenetrable waters of oblivion.

FROM "A DEMISING LOVE"

James endeavored ineffectually to ascertain the trend of her affections: her expression remained a blank. He erroneously attributed his failure to poor skill in physiognomy and inwardly bewailed his youthful neglect of the advantages of education. While so engaged he fancied he detected in her look something significant of an interest in his personality. Could he be mistaken? No, there it was again!

Arising from his sedentary attitude to the full stature of his young manhood, he crossed the intervening Persian rug and possessed himself of her hand.

"Mabel," he inquired, "do you not experience the promptings of a dawning tenderness for one to whom you are much?"

Receiving no negative answer he kissed her simultaneously on both cheeks, and, falling rapidly upon one knee, poured out his soul in beautiful language, mostly devoted to commendation of her fine character and disposition.

Mabel did not at once respond. She was deceased.

FROM "MARCH HARES"

Mrs. Rorqual deposited her embroidery on the sofa by her side and, slightly changing color, said, "No, my ideals are not unchangeable; they have undergone memorable alteration within the last hour."

"Let us hope," said D'Anchovi, uncrossing his hands, and putting one forefinger into a buttonhole of his coat, "that they are still high."

She resumed her embroidery and, looking at a painting of the martyrdom of St. Denis over the mantel, replied, "Would it matter?"

"Surely," said he, lightly beating the carpet with the

heel of his well-fitting shoe; "for ideals are more than thoughts. I sometimes think they are things—that *we* are *their* thoughts."

She did not immediately reply. A curtain at an open window moved audibly. A sunbeam crept through the lattice of the piazza outside and fell upon the window-ledge. The fly previously mentioned now walked indolently along the top of the Japanese screen, then fearlessly descended the face of it to within an inch of the mouth of a painted frog. D'Anchovi, with a lifting of his eyebrows, maintained a determined silence.

"I should think that an uncomfortable creed," Mrs. Rorqual said at last, withdrawing the tip of her shoe, which had been visible beneath the edge of her gown, and shifting her gaze from St. Denis to one of the crystal ornaments of the candelabrum pendent from the ceiling.

He passed the fingers of his right hand through his hair, slightly shifted his position on his chair and said: "Mrs. Rorqual, I have to thank you for a most agreeable hour. Shall I see you on the golf-links to-morrow?"

So they parted, but when he was gone she toyed thoughtfully with a spray of heliotrope growing in a jardinière and then ran her forefinger along a part of the pattern of the wallpaper.

FROM "A STUDY IN DISSECTION"

Captain Gerard introspected. He spread his heart, as it were, upon the dissecting-table of conscience and examined it from several points of view. It is a familiar act—we call it analysis of motive. When he had concluded he knew why he had accepted the invitation of the countess to dinner. He knew why he had insulted the count. Equally obvious were his reasons for mentioning to Iphigeneia the holy bonds of matrimony. In all his conduct since his last introspection but one act baffled him: why, alas, had he spoken to Iphigeneia of the bar-semester in his crest?

As he pondered this inexplicable problem a footfall fell upon his ear and he shuddered as if the hand of death had stepped in.

It was the countess!

FROM "HER DIPLODOCUS"

"Sir!" Miss Athylton drew herself up to her full height and looked her interlocutor squarely in the visage. For an instant he returned her scrutiny; then his eyes fell to the earth, stammering apologies. With a sweeping curtsey she passed out of the room, hand over hand.

FROM "L'AFFAIRE SMITH"

As they sat there wrapping their arms about each other, she advanced the belief that they had loved in a former state of existence.

"But not as now, Irene, surely not as now."

She was well content to let him feel so about it, and did not seek to alter the character of his emotion. To have done so would have cut her to the heart. On the contrary, a little bird perched in the passion-vine above them and sang several thrilling passages.

FROM "CLARISSE"

He gazed into her beautiful eyes for a considerable period, during which he did not converse; then he said, with an effort to be sociable: "It has been represented to me that you are a lady of great wealth. May I inquire if I have been rightly informed?"

Blushing energetically at the compliment, she replied in silence, and for a few minutes there was an embarrassing hiatus in the exchange of thought and feeling.

Fearing that he had offended her, the duke arose, and striding to the grand piano began to improvise diligently. At that moment there came in through the open window a sound of wheels on the gravel outside.

He ceased in the middle of a nocturne and would have left the room, but she restrained him:

"It is only my father returning from India," smiled she; "I shall be so glad to introduce you."

The full horror of the situation burst upon him like a thunderbolt out of a clean sky.

"Madam," he thundered, "your father is dead! He died of the plague in Bombay, and I attended the funeral, although he had cursed me with his last breath. I cannot—cannot meet him!"

With those words falling from his white lips he flung himself out of the room. A servant entered and handed Clarisse the visiting card of Mrs. Delahanty.

FROM "MARY ANN & CO."

As they neared each other on the narrow bridge Paul observed that she was profoundly agitated.

"Darling," he said, "please to signify the cause of your perturbation. It is not impossible that I may be able to remove it. You know," he added, "that I have studied medicine."

She blushed deeply, then turned pale and continued to tremble. He seized her hand and laid two fingers upon her wrist.

"The pulse," he said, "is abnormally frequent and irregular."

With a barely audible expression of disapproval, she withdrew her hand and endeavored to pass him on the narrow footway of the bridge. A misstep precipitated her into the stream, from which with no small difficulty she was taken in a dying condition, a half-mile below. The person that drew her forth from the waters was Paul's aged uncle.

"Tell Paul Dessard," she said with her last breath, "that I love him, die for him! Tell him how I strove successfully to hide my love from him lest he think me unmaidenly; but it cannot matter now if he know it. Tell him all, I pray you tell him all, and add that in that Better Land whither I go my spirit will await him with impatience, prepared to explain all."

The good old man bent over her, placed his open hand behind his ear and ejaculated:

"Hay?"

She shook her head with an infinite pathos and suspired.

FROM "IDEALS"

Where the grand old Hudson river rolls its floods seaward between the rugged Palisades and the agricultural country of its eastern bank Janey Sewell dwelt in a little vine-covered cottage in one of the most picturesque spots of the latter.

Janey was beautiful all day long. Her hair was as dark as the pinion of a crow, and her brown eyes rivaled in lustre the sheen of the sunlight on the bosom of the river. She was also a fine French scholar.

Janey's parents had dwelt in Yonkers from time immemorial, and sweet to her was her native environment, whence no proffers of a marriage into the aristocracy or nobility of England could entice her. Many coroneted hearts had been flung at her feet—many were the impassionate pleas that ducal lips had poured into her ear; she remained fancy free, determined to bestow her affection upon some worthy member of an American labor union or die a maid. We shall see with what indomitable tenacity she adhered through disheartening trials to that commendable policy.

FROM "OOPSIE MERCER"

For a long time—it seemed an eternity—they sat there hand in hand, in the gloaming. The sheep-bells tinkled faintly in the glen, and from an adjacent thicket the whip-poor-will sang rapturously. The katydid grated out her mysterious accusation from the branch of an oak overhead; the cricket droned among the glow-worms underfoot. All these vocal efforts were conspicuously futile; in their newly found happiness the lovers heeded nothing but each other. O love!

Suddenly, on the dew-starred sward, a loud oath rang out behind them. Harold rose promptly to his own feet, the lady remaining in session on the log, her hands demurely folded in her lap. The report of a firearm illuminated the gloom, and ere Harold could intercept the deadly missile it had pierced Miss Mercer's heart! She fell forward and died without medical assistance.

Harold mounted the log and obtained a fairly good view of the aggressor; it was James Wroth, and he was engaged in taking a second aim. With the lightning-like intuition of a brave man in an emergency Harold inferred that he was the intended victim.

"Fiend!" sprang he, and a death struggle was inaugurated without delay.

Let us go back to the time when we left James Wroth nourishing the fires of an intellectual tempest implanted by Miss Mercer's rejection of his suit, and embarking for Europe in another tongue.

FROM "LANCE AND LUTE"

The faint booming of the distant cannon grew more and more deafening; the thunder of the charging cavalry reverberated o'er the field of battle: the enemies were evidently making a stand.

Plympton arrived at the scene of action just as the commanding general ordered an advance along the entire front. Spurring his steed to the centre of the line he rang out his voice in accents of defiance and was promoted for gallantry.

Bertram, who was an eye-witness, immediately withdrew his objection to the marriage. This took place shortly afterward and was attended with the happiest results.

FROM "SUNDRY HEARTS"

When presented to the object of his devotion the earl could not suppress his sentiments. The Lady Gwendolin saw them as plainly as if they had been branded upon his brow. Her agitation was comparable to his. All the pent-up emotion of her deep, womanly nature surged to her countenance and paralyzed her so that she was unable to offer her hand. She consequently contented herself with a graceful inclination of the head. The earl was excessively disappointed. Turning upon his heel he bowed and walked away.

Gwendolin retired to the conservatory and uttered a deep-drawn sigh, then, returning to the ballroom, flung herself into the waltz with an assumed ectasy that elicited wide comment.

FROM "LA BELLE DAMN"

Under the harvest moon, now at its best, the corpse of Ronald showed ghastly white, the frost sparkling in its beard and hair. Clementine's consciousness of its impulchritude was without a flaw. Had she ever really experienced an un-common, an exceptional, tenderness for an object boasting so little charm? She was hardly able to take that view of the matter. All seemed unreal, indistinct and charged with dubiety. A sudden rustling in the circumjacent vegetation startled her from her dream, suggesting considerations of personal safety. Surveying the body for the last time, she impelled the stiletto into a contiguous tarn and left the scene with measured tread.

FROM "THE RECRUDESCENCE OF SQUOLLANDER"

"Clifford," said Isabel, earnestly yet softly, "are you sure that you truly love me?"

Clifford presented such testimony and evidence as he could command, and requested her decision on the sufficiency of what he had advanced.

"Oh, Clifford," she said, laying her two little hands in one of his comparatively large ones, "you have extirpated my ultimate uncertainty."

IN MOTLEY

THE A. L. C. B.

A society of which I am the proud and happy founder is the American League for the Circumvention of Bores. With a view to enlisting the reader's interest and favor and obtaining his initiation fee, I beg leave to expound the ends and methods of the order.

The League purposes to work within the law: Bores can be circumvented by killing; which may be called the circumvention direct; but for every Bore that is killed arises a swarm of Bores (reporters, lawyers, jurors, etc.) whom one is unable to kill. The League plan is humane, simple, ingenious and effective. It leaves the Bore alive, to suffer the lasting torments of his own esteem.

The American League for the Circumvention of Bores has the customary machinery of grips, pass-words, signs, a goat, solemn ceremonials and mystic hoodooing; but for practical use it employs only the Signal of Eminent Distress, to preservation of the secret whereof members are bound by the most horrible oath known to the annals of juration. It is a law that any member duly convicted in the secret tribunals of the League of failing promptly to respond to the Signal of Eminent Distress shall suffer evisceration through the nose.

The plan works this way: I am, say, on a ferry-boat. Carelessly glancing about, I see—yes, it must have been—ah!

again: the Signal of Eminent Distress! A Brother of the League is *in articulo mortis*—the demon hath him—the beak of the Bore is crimson in his heart! I go to the rescue, choosing, according to my judgment and tact, one of the Ten Thousand Forms of Benign Relief which I have memorized from the Ritual.

"Ah, my dear fellow," I perhaps say to the victim, whom I may never have seen before, "I have been looking all over the boat for you. I must have a word with you on a most important matter if your friend"—looking at the baffled Bore who has been talking into him—"will have the goodness to excuse you."

Possibly, though, I say to the signaling victim: "Sir, pardon me, but is not your name—?"

"Jonesmith," he replies, coldly; "may I ask—?"

"Ah, yes; I hope you will not think me intrusive, but a gentleman on the lower deck, who says he is your uncle, has fallen and broken his neck."

As Mr. Jonesmith with a grateful look moves off, the Bore, full of solicitude, starts to follow for assistance and condolence. I lay my hand on his arm. "Pardon, sir; the physician prescribes absolute quiet: the splendor, charm and vivacity of your conversation would unduly excite the patient."

Before the wretch can round-up his faculties the Brother in Distress has escaped and I am walking away with the 368th Aspect of Superb Unconcern, as laid down in the Ritual.

The League has been in existence in New York City for about six months. There is a younger branch at Hohokus, and another is forming at Podunk. I am the Supreme Imperial Inimitable, though every member has high rank and office. Applications for membership must be made personally to the Grand Dictatorial Caboodle, which will judge whether the applicant is himself a Bore.

A CATALOGUE OF SELECTED DOVER BOOKS
IN ALL FIELDS OF INTEREST

A CATALOG OF SELECTED DOVER
BOOKS IN ALL FIELDS OF INTEREST

THE ART NOUVEAU STYLE, edited by Roberta Waddell. 579 rare photographs of works in jewelry, metalwork, glass, ceramics, textiles, architecture and furniture by 175 artists—Mucha, Seguy, Lalique, Tiffany, many others. 288pp. 8⅜ × 11¼.
23515-7 Pa. $9.95

AMERICAN COUNTRY HOUSES OF THE GILDED AGE (Sheldon's "Artistic Country-Seats"), A. Lewis. All of Sheldon's fascinating and historically important photographs and plans. New text by Arnold Lewis. Approx. 200 illustrations. 128pp. 9⅜ × 12¼.
24301-X Pa. $7.95

THE WAY WE LIVE NOW, Anthony Trollope. Trollope's late masterpiece, marks shift to bitter satire. Character Melmotte "his greatest villain." Reproduced from original edition with 40 illustrations. 416pp. 6⅛ × 9¼.
24360-5 Pa. $7.95

BENCHLEY LOST AND FOUND, Robert Benchley. Finest humor from early 30's, about pet peeves, child psychologists, post office and others. Mostly unavailable elsewhere. 73 illustrations by Peter Arno and others. 183pp. 5⅜ × 8½.
22410-4 Pa. $3.50

ISOMETRIC PERSPECTIVE DESIGNS AND HOW TO CREATE THEM, John Locke. Isometric perspective is the picture of an object adrift in imaginary space. 75 mindboggling designs. 52pp. 8¼ × 11.
24123-8 Pa. $2.75

PERSPECTIVE FOR ARTISTS, Rex Vicat Cole. Depth, perspective of sky and sea, shadows, much more, not usually covered. 391 diagrams, 81 reproductions of drawings and paintings. 279pp. 5⅜ × 8½.
22487-2 Pa. $4.00

MOVIE-STAR PORTRAITS OF THE FORTIES, edited by John Kobal. 163 glamor, studio photos of 106 stars of the 1940s: Rita Hayworth, Ava Gardner, Marlon Brando, Clark Gable, many more. 176pp. 8⅜ × 11¼.
23546-7 Pa. $6.95

STARS OF THE BROADWAY STAGE, 1940-1967, Fred Fehl. Marlon Brando, Uta Hagen, John Kerr, John Gielgud, Jessica Tandy in great shows—*South Pacific, Galileo, West Side Story*, more. 240 black-and-white photos. 144pp. 8⅜ × 11¼.
24398-2 Pa. $8.95

ILLUSTRATED DICTIONARY OF HISTORIC ARCHITECTURE, edited by Cyril M. Harris. Extraordinary compendium of clear, concise definitions for over 5000 important architectural terms complemented by over 2000 line drawings. 592pp. 7½ × 9⅜.
24444-X Pa. $14.95

THE EARLY WORK OF FRANK LLOYD WRIGHT, F.L. Wright. 207 rare photos of Oak Park period, first great buildings: Unity Temple, Dana house, Larkin factory. Complete photos of Wasmuth edition. New Introduction. 160pp. 8⅜ × 11¼.
24381-8 Pa. $7.95

LIVING MY LIFE, Emma Goldman. Candid, no holds barred account by foremost American anarchist: her own life, anarchist movement, famous contemporaries, ideas and their impact. 944pp. 5⅜ × 8½. 22543-7, 22544-5 Pa., Two-vol. set $13.00

UNDERSTANDING THERMODYNAMICS, H.C. Van Ness. Clear, lucid treatment of first and second laws of thermodynamics. Excellent supplement to basic textbook in undergraduate science or engineering class. 103pp. 5⅜ × 8.
63277-6 Pa. $3.50

KEYBOARD WORKS FOR SOLO INSTRUMENTS, G.F. Handel. 35 neglected works from Handel's vast oeuvre, originally jotted down as improvisations. Includes Eight Great Suites, others. New sequence. 174pp. 9⅜ × 12¼.
24338-9 Pa. $7.50

AMERICAN LEAGUE BASEBALL CARD CLASSICS, Bert Randolph Sugar. 82 stars from 1900s to 60s on facsimile cards. Ruth, Cobb, Mantle, Williams, plus advertising, info, no duplications. Perforated, detachable. 16pp. 8¼ × 11.
24286-2 Pa. $2.95

A TREASURY OF CHARTED DESIGNS FOR NEEDLEWORKERS, Georgia Gorham and Jeanne Warth. 141 charted designs: owl, cat with yarn, tulips, piano, spinning wheel, covered bridge, Victorian house and many others. 48pp. 8¼ × 11.
23558-0 Pa. $1.95

DANISH FLORAL CHARTED DESIGNS, Gerda Bengtsson. Exquisite collection of over 40 different florals: anemone, Iceland poppy, wild fruit, pansies, many others. 45 illustrations. 48pp. 8¼ × 11.
23957-8 Pa. $1.75

OLD PHILADELPHIA IN EARLY PHOTOGRAPHS 1839-1914, Robert F. Looney. 215 photographs: panoramas, street scenes, landmarks, President-elect Lincoln's visit, 1876 Centennial Exposition, much more. 230pp. 8⅜ × 11¼.
23345-6 Pa. $9.95

PRELUDE TO MATHEMATICS, W.W. Sawyer. Noted mathematician's lively, stimulating account of non-Euclidean geometry, matrices, determinants, group theory, other topics. Emphasis on novel, striking aspects. 224pp. 5⅜ × 8½.
24401-6 Pa. $4.50

ADVENTURES WITH A MICROSCOPE, Richard Headstrom. 59 adventures with clothing fibers, protozoa, ferns and lichens, roots and leaves, much more. 142 illustrations. 232pp. 5⅜ × 8½.
23471-1 Pa. $3.95

IDENTIFYING ANIMAL TRACKS: MAMMALS, BIRDS, AND OTHER ANIMALS OF THE EASTERN UNITED STATES, Richard Headstrom. For hunters, naturalists, scouts, nature-lovers. Diagrams of tracks, tips on identification. 128pp. 5⅜ × 8.
24442-3 Pa. $3.50

VICTORIAN FASHIONS AND COSTUMES FROM HARPER'S BAZAR, 1867-1898, edited by Stella Blum. Day costumes, evening wear, sports clothes, shoes, hats, other accessories in over 1,000 detailed engravings. 320pp. 9⅜ × 12¼.
22990-4 Pa. $10.95

EVERYDAY FASHIONS OF THE TWENTIES AS PICTURED IN SEARS AND OTHER CATALOGS, edited by Stella Blum. Actual dress of the Roaring Twenties, with text by Stella Blum. Over 750 illustrations, captions. 156pp. 9 × 12.
24134-3 Pa. $8.50

HALL OF FAME BASEBALL CARDS, edited by Bert Randolph Sugar. Cy Young, Ted Williams, Lou Gehrig, and many other Hall of Fame greats on 92 full-color, detachable reprints of early baseball cards. No duplication of cards with *Classic Baseball Cards.* 16pp. 8¼ × 11.
23624-2 Pa. $3.50

THE ART OF HAND LETTERING, Helm Wotzkow. Course in hand lettering, Roman, Gothic, Italic, Block, Script. Tools, proportions, optical aspects, individual variation. Very quality conscious. Hundreds of specimens. 320pp. 5⅜ × 8½.
21797-3 Pa. $4.95

HOW THE OTHER HALF LIVES, Jacob A. Riis. Journalistic record of filth, degradation, upward drive in New York immigrant slums, shops, around 1900. New edition includes 100 original Riis photos, monuments of early photography. 233pp. 10 × 7⅞. 22012-5 Pa. $7.95

CHINA AND ITS PEOPLE IN EARLY PHOTOGRAPHS, John Thomson. In 200 black-and-white photographs of exceptional quality photographic pioneer Thomson captures the mountains, dwellings, monuments and people of 19th-century China. 272pp. 9⅜ × 12¼. 24393-1 Pa. $12.95

GODEY COSTUME PLATES IN COLOR FOR DECOUPAGE AND FRAMING, edited by Eleanor Hasbrouk Rawlings. 24 full-color engravings depicting 19th-century Parisian haute couture. Printed on one side only. 56pp. 8¼ × 11. 23879-2 Pa. $3.95

ART NOUVEAU STAINED GLASS PATTERN BOOK, Ed Sibbett, Jr. 104 projects using well-known themes of Art Nouveau: swirling forms, florals, peacocks, and sensuous women. 60pp. 8¼ × 11. 23577-7 Pa. $3.50

QUICK AND EASY PATCHWORK ON THE SEWING MACHINE: Susan Aylsworth Murwin and Suzzy Payne. Instructions, diagrams show exactly how to machine sew 12 quilts. 48pp. of templates. 50 figures. 80pp. 8¼ × 11. 23770-2 Pa. $3.50

THE STANDARD BOOK OF QUILT MAKING AND COLLECTING, Marguerite Ickis. Full information, full-sized patterns for making 46 traditional quilts, also 150 other patterns. 483 illustrations. 273pp. 6⅞ × 9⅝. 20582-7 Pa. $5.95

LETTERING AND ALPHABETS, J. Albert Cavanagh. 85 complete alphabets lettered in various styles; instructions for spacing, roughs, brushwork. 121pp. 8¾ × 8. 20053-1 Pa. $3.95

LETTER FORMS: 110 COMPLETE ALPHABETS, Frederick Lambert. 110 sets of capital letters; 16 lower case alphabets; 70 sets of numbers and other symbols. 110pp. 8⅛ × 11. 22872-X Pa. $4.50

ORCHIDS AS HOUSE PLANTS, Rebecca Tyson Northen. Grow cattleyas and many other kinds of orchids—in a window, in a case, or under artificial light. 63 illustrations. 148pp. 5⅜ × 8½. 23261-1 Pa. $2.95

THE MUSHROOM HANDBOOK, Louis C.C. Krieger. Still the best popular handbook. Full descriptions of 259 species, extremely thorough text, poisons, folklore, etc. 32 color plates; 126 other illustrations. 560pp. 5⅜ × 8½. 21861-9 Pa. $8.50

THE DORÉ BIBLE ILLUSTRATIONS, Gustave Doré. All wonderful, detailed plates: Adam and Eve, Flood, Babylon, life of Jesus, etc. Brief King James text with each plate. 241 plates. 241pp. 9 × 12. 23004-X Pa. $8.95

THE BOOK OF KELLS: Selected Plates in Full Color, edited by Blanche Cirker. 32 full-page plates from greatest manuscript-icon of early Middle Ages. Fantastic, mysterious. Publisher's Note. Captions. 32pp. 9⅜ × 12¼. 24345-1 Pa. $4.50

THE PERFECT WAGNERITE, George Bernard Shaw. Brilliant criticism of the Ring Cycle, with provocative interpretation of politics, economic theories behind the Ring. 136pp. 5⅜ × 8½. (Available in U.S. only) 21707-8 Pa. $3.00

THE RIME OF THE ANCIENT MARINER, Gustave Doré, S.T. Coleridge. Doré's finest work, 34 plates capture moods, subtleties of poem. Full text. 77pp. 9¼ × 12. 22305-1 Pa. $4.95

SONGS OF INNOCENCE, William Blake. The first and most popular of Blake's famous "Illuminated Books," in a facsimile edition reproducing all 31 brightly colored plates. Additional printed text of each poem. 64pp. 5¼ × 7. 22764-2 Pa. $3.50

AN INTRODUCTION TO INFORMATION THEORY, J.R. Pierce. Second (1980) edition of most impressive non-technical account available. Encoding, entropy, noisy channel, related areas, etc. 320pp. 5⅜ × 8½. 24061-4 Pa. $4.95

THE DIVINE PROPORTION: A STUDY IN MATHEMATICAL BEAUTY, H.E. Huntley. "Divine proportion" or "golden ratio" in poetry, Pascal's triangle, philosophy, psychology, music, mathematical figures, etc. Excellent bridge between science and art. 58 figures. 185pp. 5⅜ × 8½. 22254-3 Pa. $3.95

THE DOVER NEW YORK WALKING GUIDE: From the Battery to Wall Street, Mary J. Shapiro. Superb inexpensive guide to historic buildings and locales in lower Manhattan: Trinity Church, Bowling Green, more. Complete Text; maps. 36 illustrations. 48pp. 3⅞ × 9¼. 24225-0 Pa. $2.50

NEW YORK THEN AND NOW, Edward B. Watson, Edmund V. Gillon, Jr. 83 important Manhattan sites: on facing pages early photographs (1875-1925) and 1976 photos by Gillon. 172 illustrations. 171pp. 9¼ × 10. 23361-8 Pa. $7.95

HISTORIC COSTUME IN PICTURES, Braun & Schneider. Over 1450 costumed figures from dawn of civilization to end of 19th century. English captions. 125 plates. 256pp. 8⅜ × 11¼. 23150-X Pa. $7.50

VICTORIAN AND EDWARDIAN FASHION: A Photographic Survey, Alison Gernsheim. First fashion history completely illustrated by contemporary photographs. Full text plus 235 photos, 1840-1914, in which many celebrities appear. 240pp. 6½ × 9¼. 24205-6 Pa. $6.00

CHARTED CHRISTMAS DESIGNS FOR COUNTED CROSS-STITCH AND OTHER NEEDLECRAFTS, Lindberg Press. Charted designs for 45 beautiful needlecraft projects with many yuletide and wintertime motifs. 48pp. 8¼ × 11. 24356-7 Pa. $2.50

101 FOLK DESIGNS FOR COUNTED CROSS-STITCH AND OTHER NEEDLE-CRAFTS, Carter Houck. 101 authentic charted folk designs in a wide array of lovely representations with many suggestions for effective use. 48pp. 8¼ × 11. 24369-9 Pa. $2.25

FIVE ACRES AND INDEPENDENCE, Maurice G. Kains. Great back-to-the-land classic explains basics of self-sufficient farming. The one book to get. 95 illustrations. 397pp. 5⅜ × 8½. 20974-1 Pa. $4.95

A MODERN HERBAL, Margaret Grieve. Much the fullest, most exact, most useful compilation of herbal material. Gigantic alphabetical encyclopedia, from aconite to zedoary, gives botanical information, medical properties, folklore, economic uses, and much else. Indispensable to serious reader. 161 illustrations. 888pp. 6½ × 9¼. (Available in U.S. only) 22798-7, 22799-5 Pa., Two-vol. set $16.45

DECORATIVE NAPKIN FOLDING FOR BEGINNERS, Lillian Oppenheimer and Natalie Epstein. 22 different napkin folds in the shape of a heart, clown's hat, love knot, etc. 63 drawings. 48pp. 8¼ × 11. 23797-4 Pa. $1.95

DECORATIVE LABELS FOR HOME CANNING, PRESERVING, AND OTHER HOUSEHOLD AND GIFT USES, Theodore Menten. 128 gummed, perforated labels, beautifully printed in 2 colors. 12 versions. Adhere to metal, glass, wood, ceramics. 24pp. 8¼ × 11. 23219-0 Pa. $2.95

EARLY AMERICAN STENCILS ON WALLS AND FURNITURE, Janet Waring. Thorough coverage of 19th-century folk art: techniques, artifacts, surviving specimens. 166 illustrations, 7 in color. 147pp. of text. 7⅞ × 10¾. 21906-2 Pa. $9.95

AMERICAN ANTIQUE WEATHERVANES, A.B. & W.T. Westervelt. Extensively illustrated 1883 catalog exhibiting over 550 copper weathervanes and finials. Excellent primary source by one of the principal manufacturers. 104pp. 6⅛ × 9¼. 24396-6 Pa. $3.95

ART STUDENTS' ANATOMY, Edmond J. Farris. Long favorite in art schools. Basic elements, common positions, actions. Full text, 158 illustrations. 159pp. 5⅜ × 8½. 20744-7 Pa. $3.95

BRIDGMAN'S LIFE DRAWING, George B. Bridgman. More than 500 drawings and text teach you to abstract the body into its major masses. Also specific areas of anatomy. 192pp. 6½ × 9¼. (EA) 22710-3 Pa. $4.50

COMPLETE PRELUDES AND ETUDES FOR SOLO PIANO, Frederic Chopin. All 26 Preludes, all 27 Etudes by greatest composer of piano music. Authoritative Paderewski edition. 224pp. 9 × 12. (Available in U.S. only) 24052-5 Pa. $7.50

PIANO MUSIC 1888-1905, Claude Debussy. Deux Arabesques, Suite Bergamesque, Masques, 1st series of Images, etc. 9 others, in corrected editions. 175pp. 9⅜ × 12¼. (ECE) 22771-5 Pa. $5.95

TEDDY BEAR IRON-ON TRANSFER PATTERNS, Ted Menten. 80 iron-on transfer patterns of male and female Teddys in a wide variety of activities, poses, sizes. 48pp. 8¼ × 11. 24596-9 Pa. $2.25

A PICTURE HISTORY OF THE BROOKLYN BRIDGE, M.J. Shapiro. Profusely illustrated account of greatest engineering achievement of 19th century. 167 rare photos & engravings recall construction, human drama. Extensive, detailed text. 122pp. 8¼ × 11. 24403-2 Pa. $7.95

NEW YORK IN THE THIRTIES, Berenice Abbott. Noted photographer's fascinating study shows new buildings that have become famous and old sights that have disappeared forever. 97 photographs. 97pp. 11⅜ × 10. 22967-X Pa. $7.50

MATHEMATICAL TABLES AND FORMULAS, Robert D. Carmichael and Edwin R. Smith. Logarithms, sines, tangents, trig functions, powers, roots, reciprocals, exponential and hyperbolic functions, formulas and theorems. 269pp. 5⅜ × 8½. 60111-0 Pa. $4.95

HANDBOOK OF MATHEMATICAL FUNCTIONS WITH FORMULAS, GRAPHS, AND MATHEMATICAL TABLES, edited by Milton Abramowitz and Irene A. Stegun. Vast compendium: 29 sets of tables, some to as high as 20 places. 1,046pp. 8 × 10½. 61272-4 Pa. $19.95

REASON IN ART, George Santayana. Renowned philosopher's provocative, seminal treatment of basis of art in instinct and experience. Volume Four of *The Life of Reason*. 230pp. 5⅜ × 8. 24358-3 Pa. $4.50

LANGUAGE, TRUTH AND LOGIC, Alfred J. Ayer. Famous, clear introduction to Vienna, Cambridge schools of Logical Positivism. Role of philosophy, elimination of metaphysics, nature of analysis, etc. 160pp. 5⅜ × 8½. (USCO) 20010-8 Pa. $2.75

BASIC ELECTRONICS, U.S. Bureau of Naval Personnel. Electron tubes, circuits, antennas, AM, FM, and CW transmission and receiving, etc. 560 illustrations. 567pp. 6½ × 9¼. 21076-6 Pa. $8.95

THE ART DECO STYLE, edited by Theodore Menten. Furniture, jewelry, metalwork, ceramics, fabrics, lighting fixtures, interior decors, exteriors, graphics from pure French sources. Over 400 photographs. 183pp. 8⅜ × 11¼. 22824-X Pa. $6.95

THE FOUR BOOKS OF ARCHITECTURE, Andrea Palladio. 16th-century classic covers classical architectural remains, Renaissance revivals, classical orders, etc. 1738 Ware English edition. 216 plates. 110pp. of text. 9½ × 12¾. 21308-0 Pa. $11.50

THE WIT AND HUMOR OF OSCAR WILDE, edited by Alvin Redman. More than 1000 ripostes, paradoxes, wisecracks: Work is the curse of the drinking classes, I can resist everything except temptations, etc. 258pp. 5⅜ × 8½. (USCO) 20602-5 Pa. $3.95

THE DEVIL'S DICTIONARY, Ambrose Bierce. Barbed, bitter, brilliant witticisms in the form of a dictionary. Best, most ferocious satire America has produced. 145pp. 5⅜ × 8½. 20487-1 Pa. $2.50

ERTÉ'S FASHION DESIGNS, Erté. 210 black-and-white inventions from *Harper's Bazar*, 1918-32, plus 8pp. full-color covers. Captions. 88pp. 9 × 12. 24203-X Pa. $6.50

ERTÉ GRAPHICS, Erté. Collection of striking color graphics: *Seasons, Alphabet, Numerals, Aces* and *Precious Stones*. 50 plates, including 4 on covers. 48pp. 9⅜ × 12¼. 23580-7 Pa. $6.95

PAPER FOLDING FOR BEGINNERS, William D. Murray and Francis J. Rigney. Clearest book for making origami sail boats, roosters, frogs that move legs, etc. 40 projects. More than 275 illustrations. 94pp. 5⅜ × 8½. 20713-7 Pa. $2.25

ORIGAMI FOR THE ENTHUSIAST, John Montroll. Fish, ostrich, peacock, squirrel, rhinoceros, Pegasus, 19 other intricate subjects. Instructions. Diagrams. 128pp. 9 × 12. 23799-0 Pa. $4.95

CROCHETING NOVELTY POT HOLDERS, edited by Linda Macho. 64 useful, whimsical pot holders feature kitchen themes, animals, flowers, other novelties. Surprisingly easy to crochet. Complete instructions. 48pp. 8¼ × 11. 24296-X Pa. $1.95

CROCHETING DOILIES, edited by Rita Weiss. Irish Crochet, Jewel, Star Wheel, Vanity Fair and more. Also luncheon and console sets, runners and centerpieces. 51 illustrations. 48pp. 8¼ × 11. 23424-X Pa. $2.50

YUCATAN BEFORE AND AFTER THE CONQUEST, Diego de Landa. Only significant account of Yucatan written in the early post-Conquest era. Translated by William Gates. Over 120 illustrations. 162pp. 5⅜ × 8½. 23622-6 Pa. $3.50

ORNATE PICTORIAL CALLIGRAPHY, E.A. Lupfer. Complete instructions, over 150 examples help you create magnificent "flourishes" from which beautiful animals and objects gracefully emerge. 8⅛ × 11. 21957-7 Pa. $2.95

DOLLY DINGLE PAPER DOLLS, Grace Drayton. Cute chubby children by same artist who did Campbell Kids. Rare plates from 1910s. 30 paper dolls and over 100 outfits reproduced in full color. 32pp. 9¼ × 12¼. 23711-7 Pa. $3.50

CURIOUS GEORGE PAPER DOLLS IN FULL COLOR, H. A. Rey, Kathy Allert. Naughty little monkey-hero of children's books in two doll figures, plus 48 full-color costumes: pirate, Indian chief, fireman, more. 32pp. 9¼ × 12¼.
24386-9 Pa. $3.50

GERMAN: HOW TO SPEAK AND WRITE IT, Joseph Rosenberg. Like *French, How to Speak and Write It.* Very rich modern course, with a wealth of pictorial material. 330 illustrations. 384pp. 5⅜ × 8½. (USUKO) 20271-2 Pa. $4.75

CATS AND KITTENS: 24 Ready-to-Mail Color Photo Postcards, D. Holby. Handsome collection; feline in a variety of adorable poses. Identifications. 12pp. on postcard stock. 8¼ × 11. 24469-5 Pa. $2.95

MARILYN MONROE PAPER DOLLS, Tom Tierney. 31 full-color designs on heavy stock, from *The Asphalt Jungle, Gentlemen Prefer Blondes,* 22 others. 1 doll. 16 plates. 32pp. 9⅜ × 12¼. 23769-9 Pa. $3.50

FUNDAMENTALS OF LAYOUT, F.H. Wills. All phases of layout design discussed and illustrated in 121 illustrations. Indispensable as student's text or handbook for professional. 124pp. 8⅛ × 11. 21279-3 Pa. $4.50

FANTASTIC SUPER STICKERS, Ed Sibbett, Jr. 75 colorful pressure-sensitive stickers. Peel off and place for a touch of pizzazz: clowns, penguins, teddy bears, etc. Full color. 16pp. 8¼ × 11. 24471-7 Pa. $2.95

LABELS FOR ALL OCCASIONS, Ed Sibbett, Jr. 6 labels each of 16 different designs—baroque, art nouveau, art deco, Pennsylvania Dutch, etc.—in full color. 24pp. 8¼ × 11. 23688-9 Pa. $2.95

HOW TO CALCULATE QUICKLY: RAPID METHODS IN BASIC MATHE-MATICS, Henry Sticker. Addition, subtraction, multiplication, division, checks, etc. More than 8000 problems, solutions. 185pp. 5 × 7¼. 20295-X Pa. $2.95

THE CAT COLORING BOOK, Karen Baldauski. Handsome, realistic renderings of 40 splendid felines, from American shorthair to exotic types. 44 plates. Captions. 48pp. 8¼ × 11. 24011-8 Pa. $2.25

THE TALE OF PETER RABBIT, Beatrix Potter. The inimitable Peter's terrifying adventure in Mr. McGregor's garden, with all 27 wonderful, full-color Potter illustrations. 55pp. 4¼ × 5½. (Available in U.S. only) 22827-4 Pa. $1.75

BASIC ELECTRICITY, U.S. Bureau of Naval Personnel. Batteries, circuits, conductors, AC and DC, inductance and capacitance, generators, motors, trans-formers, amplifiers, etc. 349 illustrations. 448pp. 6½ × 9¼. 20973-3 Pa. $7.95

READY-TO-USE BORDERS, Ted Menten. Both traditional and unusual interchangeable borders in a tremendous array of sizes, shapes, and styles. 32 plates. 64pp. 8¼ × 11. 23782-6 Pa. $3.50

THE WHOLE CRAFT OF SPINNING, Carol Kroll. Preparing fiber, drop spindle, treadle wheel, other fibers, more. Highly creative, yet simple. 43 illustrations. 48pp. 8¼ × 11. 23968-3 Pa. $2.50

HIDDEN PICTURE PUZZLE COLORING BOOK, Anna Pomaska. 31 delightful pictures to color with dozens of objects, people and animals hidden away to find. Captions. Solutions. 48pp. 8¼ × 11. 23909-8 Pa. $2.25

QUILTING WITH STRIPS AND STRINGS, H.W. Rose. Quickest, easiest way to turn left-over fabric into handsome quilt. 46 patchwork quilts; 31 full-size templates. 48pp. 8¼ × 11. 24357-5 Pa. $3.25

NATURAL DYES AND HOME DYEING, Rita J. Adrosko. Over 135 specific recipes from historical sources for cotton, wool, other fabrics. Genuine premodern handicrafts. 12 illustrations. 160pp. 5⅜ × 8½. 22688-3 Pa. $2.95

CARVING REALISTIC BIRDS, H.D. Green. Full-sized patterns, step-by-step instructions for robins, jays, cardinals, finches, etc. 97 illustrations. 80pp. 8¼ × 11. 23484-3 Pa. $3.00

GEOMETRY, RELATIVITY AND THE FOURTH DIMENSION, Rudolf Rucker. Exposition of fourth dimension, concepts of relativity as Flatland characters continue adventures. Popular, easily followed yet accurate, profound. 141 illustrations. 133pp. 5⅜ × 8½. 23400-2 Pa. $3.00

READY-TO-USE SMALL FRAMES AND BORDERS, Carol B. Grafton. Graphic message? Frame it graphically with 373 new frames and borders in many styles: Art Nouveau, Art Deco, Op Art. 64pp. 8¼ × 11. 24375-3 Pa. $3.50

CELTIC ART: THE METHODS OF CONSTRUCTION, George Bain. Simple geometric techniques for making Celtic interlacements, spirals, Kellstype initials, animals, humans, etc. Over 500 illustrations. 160pp. 9 × 12. (Available in U.S. only) 22923-8 Pa. $6.00

THE TALE OF TOM KITTEN, Beatrix Potter. Exciting text and all 27 vivid, full-color illustrations to charming tale of naughty little Tom getting into mischief again. 58pp. 4¼ × 5½. (USO) 24502-0 Pa. $1.75

WOODEN PUZZLE TOYS, Ed Sibbett, Jr. Transfer patterns and instructions for 24 easy-to-do projects: fish, butterflies, cats, acrobats, Humpty Dumpty, 19 others. 48pp. 8¼ × 11. 23713-3 Pa. $2.50

MY FAMILY TREE WORKBOOK, Rosemary A. Chorzempa. Enjoyable, easy-to-use introduction to genealogy designed specially for children. Data pages plus text. Instructive, educational, valuable. 64pp. 8¼ × 11. 24229-3 Pa. $2.50

Prices subject to change without notice.
Available at your book dealer or write for free catalog to Dept. GI, Dover Publications, Inc., 31 East 2nd St. Mineola, N.Y. 11501. Dover publishes more than 175 books each year on science, elementary and advanced mathematics, biology, music, art, literary history, social sciences and other areas.